Confident Networking

for Career Success and Satisfaction

Gael Lindenfield & Stuart Lindenfield

PIATKUS

First published in Great Britain in 2005 by
Piatkus Books Ltd
5 Windmill Street
London W1T 2JA
email: info@piatkus.co.uk

A catalogue record for this book is available from the British Library

ISBN 0 7499 2650 3

This book has been printed on paper manufactured with respect for the environment using wood from managed sustainable resources

Illustrations by Jessica Stockham
Text design by Paul Saunders
Edited by Carol Franklin

Typeset by Phoenix Photosetting, Lordswood, Chatham, Kent
Printed and bound in Great Britain by
Antony Rowe Ltd, Chippenham, Wiltshire

As in all other walks of life successful networking is vital to career progression. I hear time and time again people complaining that others advance because of who they know. Of course they do – it was always and always will be so. The moral? Get to know those who can help....this is simply a process of selling yourself – the most difficult kind of selling. It requires a great deal of confidence to do it effectively and this book will help to improve your skills in this vital area.

Sir Gerry Robinson – Non-Executive Chairman of Allied Domecq. Formerly Chairman of Arts Council England, Granada, British Sky Broadcasting Group and ITN.

Confident Networking *acutely and accurately observes the intricacies of this essential but often overlooked tool for business success. Its clear and practical advice will be invaluable for those who think they lack the confidence to network successfully, as well as for old lags at the game who will find new tricks to learn.*

Russell Grossman – Head of Internal Communications, BBC

An excellent guide for people new to the art and those who, have been avid practitioners for many years …extremely relevant, entertaining and easy to read … a major area for learning for me was the section on e-networking. The book highlights its power and explains in straightforward terms how to access and benefit from it.

Manus Fullerton – Executive Director, Lloyds TSB

Undeniably compelling and an excellent road map for anyone tackling the challenge of 'it's not what you know, it's who you know.' Gael Lindenfield and Stuart Lindenfield have nailed a huge problem and provided the solution in one fell swoop. The pressure to succeed at networking has never been greater. Their timing with Confident Networking *is impeccable.*

Susan Steele – Global Head of Professional Resourcing, Linklaters

I liked the use of the animals with alliteration – great for visualising … helps you to see that networking is not an art for the confident few …. Confident Networking *is a great everyday tool to have around and dip into for tips and refreshers.*

Ruth Altman – Director of Human Resources, Cranfield University

What a great read! I've really enjoyed discovering some wonderful and practical tips … those on making good, relevant and positive conversation should help me when I next walk into a room full of business contacts feeling nervous in spite of looking outwardly confident!

Karen Warden – Head of Professional & Executive Development, the Institute of Financial Services

A hugely valuable book for anyone who wants to learn or improve networking skills … neatly combines the psychological, professional and cultural aspects of networking and suffuses them with empathy for the reader and passion for the possibilities offered by networking, the quintessential 21st-century business skill.

Ezri Carlebach – Head of Communications, RSA; former president, International Association of Business Communicators, UK.

Full of great tips and practical advice, this book will undoubtedly help anyone who wants to gain confidence and make more from their networking opportunities.

Sandra Morris – Human Resources Manager, Vodafone Group Services

Gael and Stuart Lindenfield, drawing on their extensive experience as consultants and writers, demystify the process of networking ....packed with case examples and written in an engaging and straightforward style, the book will be essential reading for anyone wishing to become an effective networker.

Dr Linda Holbeche, Director of Research & Strategy, Roffey Park Institute

Packed with an abundance of real examples and tips ....this book allays fears tremendously by making the experience of networking fun, and provides the tools for beginning successful networking. For the experienced networker it tackles the challenges of maintaining networked relationships.

Gillian King – Global Procurement Executive, Financial Services

An excellent guide to the do's and don'ts of building a successful set of relationships .... regardless of their level of self-confidence, anyone who needs to network for business success (and who doesn't) will benefit from reading it.

Peter Thomson – Director, Future Work Forum, Henley Management College

This book and offers clear practical guidance that gives us all the opportunity to develop a critical skill and invest in the future. Read the book, put it into practice and the investment will be rewarded many times over.

Paul Gostick – International Chairman, The Chartered Institute of Marketing

I am often asked, 'How can I get the most out of networking?' For a lucky few people it just comes naturally. For most it requires effort and concentration. For some it is pure torture. This book provides a refreshing and realistic guide to help those who want to enhance their networking skills. The answer to the question will now be 'read Confident Networking*'.*

Betty Thayer – CEO, Exec-appointments.com

A practical and emotional guide... like a journey into a new world, readers learn to explore and become confident enough to join the new and old world of networking communities, both on and offline. ...this book provides the tools to set you free.

Penny Power – Founder and Director of Ecademy

To produce a book that combines the development of both the knowledge of the networking process and the qualities needed to succeed at it, is inspired! Its structure is easy to follow and includes a series of exercises that if put into practice will produce what it says on the tin – Confident Networking for Career Success and Satisfaction!

Mike Batcheler – Director of HR, Novartis Pharmaceuticals UK Ltd

Dedication

To the people of La Puebla de los Infantes, Seville Province, Spain, who have been the most inspiring and supportive community network we have ever known.

Acknowledgements

We are immensely grateful to many hundreds of friends and colleagues who have supported and advised us while we were researching this book.

In particular, we are especially indebted to Susannah Lindenfield (our daughter!), Christine Clacey, and Penny Power for their insights and constructive feedback on the text as it progressed and Jessica Stockham for her wonderful drawings of Cool Cat, Buzzy Bee and Wise Owl.

Additionally, we feel privileged to have been able to incorporate the generously shared networking wisdom of the following individuals: Scott Allen, Mike Bacheler, Simon Barker, Bruce Boxall, Allan Engelhardt, David Gilbert, Simon Graham, Konstantin Guericke, Mike Heaton, Linda Holbeche, Herminia Ibarra, Roger Jones, Bruce Lewin, Giles Long, Andy Lopata, Nick Moore, Mike Nevin, Larry Osei-Kwaku, Mark Pyman, Deric Quaile, Thomas Power, Gerry Robinson, Glenda Stone, Betty Thayer, Tiffany Thomas, Glenn Watkins, and Derek Wood.

Finally, we would like to thank Gill Bailey and her Piatkus colleagues for their enthusiastic support, highly perceptive feedback and skilled editing. They have helped to make the writing of this book an enjoyable team project.

Contents

Introduction 1

1 What networking is (and what it isn't) 13

Part One: Cool Cat Qualities 29

2 Sound self-belief 31
3 Incorruptible integrity 47
4 Resilient drive 62
5 Genuine generosity 75
6 Unashamed humility 81
7 Calculated courage 93

Part Two: Buzzy Bee Skills 103

8 Impact instantly with a lasting impression 105
9 Conversing with confidence 125
10 E-connect with magnetism 161
11 Proactively build and maintain your relationships 182
12 Assertively protect yourself and others 199
13 Build a distinctive reputation 212

Part Three: Wise Owl Know-how 227

14 Know where to connect 229
15 Know the secrets of efficiency 243

16 Know how to help others 248
17 Know how to encourage your organisations to be better connected 252
18 Know how to keep learning 259
19 Know how to network strategically 261

… And finally 265

Notes 267
Appendix 1: Useful websites 268
Appendix 2: Recommended books 272
Appendix 3: UAP form 274
Index 276

Introduction

Picture us both in the heart of the Andalusian countryside, having lunch with our Spanish friends. As usual, there were about 25 people sitting chattering over one another around an overflowing table. Out-of-the-blue, someone shouted across the room to us:

> *'So what's this new book called that you are both so busy writing?'*

We told them the title and immediately a deathly silence filled the air. It hung about embarrassingly until a kind someone rescued us with a change of subject. We were shocked. Normally, our new projects prompt a warm, enthusiastic response and endless questions. When the Spanish editions of my books appear, they speed around the hill town of La Puebla de los Infantes where we have had a house for 15 years.

So why did the news of this particular book fall so flat with our friends in Spain? We think it was because networking just isn't an issue there – it's a way of life. It's taken for granted. It is, after all, the only way anyone ever can do successful business or establish a paying career in this small, rural community. Indeed, survival itself depends upon having and maintaining a strong, mutually supportive web of social relationships. The means of doing this from customary lengthy street chats through to elaborate community rituals are firmly ingrained in everyday life. That's why the 'strange' idea of reading a book on the subject stunned our friends into unusual silence. No doubt we would have met a similar reaction in small, interdependent villages and towns all over the world.

In contrast, in our other life in the competitive and cosmopolitan heart of London, we have experienced no difficulty in explaining our reasons for writing this book. Here, as in most large urban cities, cradle-to-grave jobs no longer exist; employers are sometimes 8,000 miles away and neighbours might not know each other's names, let alone be willing or able to help each other with business or work contacts. On the other hand, the business gurus and career coaches are saying loud and clear that who you know is fast becoming even more important than what you know. Recent research has revealed, first, that the foundations for business and other kinds of career success now depend more than ever on having a strong web of both internal and external work connections. Secondly, it has indicated that the ability to build and maintain such a web is one of today's key competencies for successful career development.

So, not surprisingly, in such relatively socially isolated working environments there is a growing thirst for knowledge on how to network. My husband, Stuart, being immersed in the career transition world, was ahead of me in spotting this trend. Moreover, as an outgoing extrovert, he welcomed it. He was thrilled to have the excuse to spend more time in his element. After some heavy nagging, he succeeded in dragging me (an introvert and so less naturally inclined) along to one of the bumper networking events that are now a growing feature of London business life. I was reluctantly impressed. The buzz was infectious and real. This was not just schmoozing and boozing for hedonistic pleasure. Significant meaningful relationships were being formed and enjoyed. I could not deny that networking was making a big difference to vast numbers of people's working lives. I heard success story after success story about how ideal jobs and new customers had been found, mutually beneficial business alliances forged and difficult recruitment problems solved. (Not to mention the development of great new friendships.)

After several months of attending events, networking on internet clubs and reading extensively around the subject, the seeds of this book began to sprout. I was keen to understand what kind of people made good networkers and wondered if self-confidence was an issue. So, I set about meeting hundreds of dedicated and successful people of all ages and in many different areas of work and at differing stages of the career track. I also started an internet club on Ecademy, the online business networking platform. It is called The Confidence Club and is a forum and meeting place for people interested in the issue of confidence. It also offers support, advice and group meetings for networkers who are being held back by problems associated with their own confidence.

I was surprised to observe and learn that personality predisposition was not a predictor of success. Effective networking could obviously be enjoyed and done just as well by both outgoing extroverts and shy introverts. They just did it differently. But I did, however, find that personal confidence appeared to be a crucial make or break factor. It soon became apparent that those who excelled in this new, internationally connected world were super-confident. These were the self-assured, charismatic networkers who glided effortlessly into great relationships with anyone with whom they chose to connect. Their style of interacting might vary according to their personality, but they all shared some basic characteristics of highly confident people. For example, they had strong self-belief, were socially competent and also knowledgeable.

In contrast, those people with less psychological poise and social flair were either staying on the fringes or hadn't joined this bandwagon at all. When I talked to them about networking, I found many assumed that it could never work for them. Typical explanations they gave were:

> *'I could never be any good at it because I don't have the right personality for it. I'm just not gregarious or confident enough.'*
>
> *'I'm naturally timid and find any kind of socialising too nerve-racking. That's just the way I am.'*
>
> *'I never know what to say or when to say it – I am useless at making conversation. I always seem to end up saying something stupid or embarrassing so I don't do myself any favours. You are either good at that sort of thing or you're not.'*

'I hate it – it is my idea of hell! I'll always avoid it like the plague even though I know I'm supposed to do it. You are not going to convince me to go again.'

After spending a career leading workshops and writing books on how to build and maintain self-confidence and communicate effectively, this was a challenge I couldn't resist. And neither could Stuart. He was concerned too. Through his specialist experience as a leading networking expert, he knew that psychological factors as well as interpersonal skills and know-how were holding back so many of his clients. Even those who are at the most senior executive level are frequently fearful of stepping outside their small circles of comfort to extend their web of connections.

So in spite of the potential risks to our marriage of working closely together, we embarked on this project jointly. We are now so pleased that our passionate joint determination to level the networking playing field for the less confident, superseded our fears of business meetings in bed and top-dog marital battles. We believe that by pooling our individual reservoirs of expertise in confidence and networking, and by drawing on our differing personality perspectives, we have designed a unique and highly effective self-help programme. We hope you agree after reading and working through it!

Do you need to read this book?

Here is a quick test you can do to see how near you already are to being a confident networker. Score each of the following statements using a scale from 5 down to 1, as follows:

5 = Strongly agree
4 = Agree
3 = Neither agree nor disagree
2 = Disagree
1 = Strongly disagree

	5	4	3	2	1
I enjoy meeting strangers from all walks of working life	☐	☐	☐	☐	☐
I am continually making great new and useful relationships	☐	☐	☐	☐	☐
I understand the difference between an ordinary social relationship and a business networking relationship	☐	☐	☐	☐	☐
If I wanted or needed a change of job or career, I have an address book full of names of well-connected people whom I could easily contact and who would be willing and able to help me	☐	☐	☐	☐	☐
I enjoy starting conversations with potentially interesting people	☐	☐	☐	☐	☐
I like to volunteer to speak at events or conferences	☐	☐	☐	☐	☐
I'm always finding new ways of making my network more diverse	☐	☐	☐	☐	☐
I offer suggestions for ways of improving communication in my organisation	☐	☐	☐	☐	☐
When meeting new people, I'm able to quickly convey my specialism in a matter of seconds	☐	☐	☐	☐	☐

	5	4	3	2	1
My contacts all clearly understand what I can offer	☐	☐	☐	☐	☐
I can readily bounce back from brush-offs and rejections and my own faux pas and mistakes	☐	☐	☐	☐	☐
I am not the kind of person who puts on an act to impress others	☐	☐	☐	☐	☐
I regularly engage with people from worlds of work other than my own	☐	☐	☐	☐	☐
I use the internet frequently to converse with people outside my immediate circle of friends and colleagues	☐	☐	☐	☐	☐
I can easily name at least three on-line business or social networks	☐	☐	☐	☐	☐
I stand up for myself in a calm and polite way when people are rude to me	☐	☐	☐	☐	☐
Feedback I get indicates that I'm seen as a good listener who can understand and take account of other people's points of view	☐	☐	☐	☐	☐
I am someone that people turn to when they need a useful contact	☐	☐	☐	☐	☐
I would seize an opportunity to talk to a CEO or someone famous	☐	☐	☐	☐	☐
I am often being approached by people who have heard about me and my work	☐	☐	☐	☐	☐
One of my biggest challenges is keeping up with the tide of new business referrals or new opportunities that I am continuously receiving	☐	☐	☐	☐	☐

Now add up your score and check out where you stand currently:

- If you scored **over 95**, it is highly likely that you are already a super-confident networker and the envy of many! But, to double check, you could ask somebody else to rate you for a second opinion! If the score remains the same, then you may not need this book.
- If you scored **between 80 and 94**, you are already a good networker, and if you embrace the refinements suggested in this book it could convert you to a great networker.
- If you scored **79 or less**, please stay with us throughout. We assure you that this book will help you a great deal.

How will this book help you to become a more confident networker?

This book will guide you step-by-step through a self-development programme that will build the specific aspects of inner and outer confidence plus the knowledge successful networking demands. In Chapter 1 you will gain a clear understanding of what networking is and what it isn't, and become aware of the different forms it can take. You will learn all you need to know about that crucial component for success – confidence. Finally, you will find out how your career and working life can benefit from effective networking.

The three main sections form the basis of the self-help programme designed to build the personal qualities, the social competence and the know-how of a super-confident networker. Each of the six chapters in the three main sections will contain some motivating discussion on each topic, followed by an abundance of tips, exercises and inspiring real-life stories. If you have already flicked quickly through the book, you may have noticed the presence of some strange creatures that don't usually inhabit business books. We use three animals as our 'role models' for each section: Cool Cat, Buzzy Bee and Wise Owl. We did this partly to add some fun to the programme, and partly to use their symbolism to make the key elements of confidence easier to remember. These creatures now feel like our friends and we hope you grow to love them too! Here's a brief overview of each of the three sections.

Cool Cat Qualities

In these chapters you will learn how to build and maintain your inner confidence. You will find out which are the key psychological strengths that you need to keep inwardly cool through the ups and downs of a networker's 'hunting' life. Our tips will show you how you can counter even the most deeply ingrained negative attitudes and lifestyle habits, so that you can rely on being able to stay positively motivated and bounce back from setbacks. Cool Cat Qualities are those that form the backbone of confidence, and your work on developing them will create a firm inner foundation of self-assurance and poise:

- sound self-belief
- incorruptible integrity

- resilient drive
- genuine generosity
- unashamed humility
- calculated courage.

Buzzy Bee Skills

In these chapters you will be working on your outer confidence. You will learn how to develop the core social skills you need to confidently 'cross-fertilise and pollinate' with others and buzz effortlessly around so that the connections you need and enjoy can blossom and bloom.

This is by far the longest section in the programme, but don't be daunted. The process of learning Buzzy Bee's skills is in fact much easier than it may at first appear. (And, it may also be a good deal quicker than making the more fundamental personality changes that are sometimes required for being a Cool Cat.) We have unpicked the secrets of the confident networker's charisma and interpersonal behaviour and developed easy strategies to enable you to do the following:

- impact instantly with a lasting impression
- converse with confidence
- e-connect with magnetism
- proactively build relationships

- assertively protect yourself and others
- build a distinctive reputation.

Wise Owl Know-how

These chapters will show you how to acquire the knowledge that you need to stay wised-up about the resources and opportunities available to help you network efficiently and, as a result, become even more confident. This is the shortest section of the book, but that doesn't mean it will necessarily be the shortest in your self-help programme. It is essentially a guide to further learning and the resources you could access. How long you will need to spend on it will depend on how wised-up you already are in each of these following six areas:

- where to connect
- secrets of efficiency
- how to help others
- what helps organisations become well connected
- how to keep learning
- how to network strategically.

How you can make the most of this book

We suggest that you skim-read the whole book first and mark the sections that have particular resonance for you. Half the battle in any kind of learning programme is won when you know where to start and what particular areas you need to focus on.

Once you have done this, read the book again – this time slowly, over a few months. Give yourself time to do the exercises and try out the tips and practise the strategies. Unfortunately, you cannot develop confidence or networking competence just by reading a book. You must take a great deal of action as well. But if you do both, you will be surprised at how at easy it can be to become a super-confident networker. Once you are, you too can look forward to having a personal web of diverse and stimulating relationships that you will be able to turn to at any time in your career for advice and valuable connections. And, as if that wasn't enough, a vibrant network guarantees that you will be less bored and have more fun and true friendship in your working life, as well as increased success and satisfaction.

Gael Lindenfield, August 2005

1

What networking is (and what it isn't)

OUR UNDERSTANDING OF A NETWORK is that it is a web of relationships that have the potential to be mutually helpful and mutually trusting. When you are networking, you are either building or maintaining these relationships by interacting socially with others. In business networking these relationships can appear to be very similar to social friendships, but there are some underlying differences and expectations because of the potential for them to become commercial in some form or other. In chapter 11 of the Buzzy Bee Skills section (Proactively build relationships), we shall be examining this aspect of networking in some detail.

An off-putting misconception some people have about networking is that it is a 'schmoozy', underhand form of selling. It isn't. Think of our Andalusian hill town as mentioned in the introduction. People there, as in other small, self-contained communities, do not use their network of social relationships to push their products or services on to each other. But useful commercial exchanges, working alliances and career tip-offs are continually happening within it. People have grown up knowing who does what and whom they can trust. Information about each other is also regularly updated and relationships strengthened because there are so many community activities. Furthermore, social chit-chit is a 'compulsory' prerequisite before the possibility of any deal is even discussed.

The best business and career networks function in basically the same way, even though their membership may span the globe. They all provide both formal and informal opportunities for the development of long-term social relationships between colleagues, clients and competitors. They encourage the sharing of personal and work-related information, which will build trust and facilitate the successful exchanges of goods and services whenever such needs arise. They also function as insurance against a rainy day. When you are part of such a strongly connected web of mutually supportive relationships (even internet-only based ones), you have a greater sense of personal security. You know that there will always be someone there to advise and help you meet unwelcome as well as welcome challenges.

These kinds of networks (the kind we want to help you build) are not arenas where hard-sells and manipulative marketing take place. Indeed this kind of behaviour would not be welcome at all. Experienced networkers know that it pollutes the very atmosphere that keeps their valued web of connections alive.

On the other hand, these networks are arenas in which people continually find goods and services that they want to buy, people they want to recruit and jobs and contacts they need. This is because they are a great resource of trusted information about people and what they have to offer. Members of such networks are transparently and continually on display to one another. You are expected to openly and honestly share your strengths, talents, skills, creative ideas and successes and give information about what you have available to sell. So, when any member has a need, they can quickly and easily access trustworthy advice, products and services.

Unconscious networking

It is important to be aware that networking and this kind of useful exchange of information about people can happen anywhere and at any time. It can even take place without any conscious effort on your part. For example, a chance encounter might 'throw' you together with someone and then a mutually rewarding relationship could simply evolve as you continue to have contact with each other. You almost certainly have this kind of network already, even though it may not yet be quite as good or as extensive as it could be. Consider this example. Gill, a florist, only a week ago, opened a new shop in an area she didn't know. The illustration (overleaf) shows that she already has a potentially rewarding network, without even trying to build relationships. You can see that just through coming into contact with a few people during the last week, she has a web of contacts made up of people who know people. This network could help her to find new customers and be a great new resource for many people who have previously had to buy inferior flowers from the local garage.

Strategic networking

Alternatively, you can build a network more consciously and purposefully, as you will be doing throughout this programme.

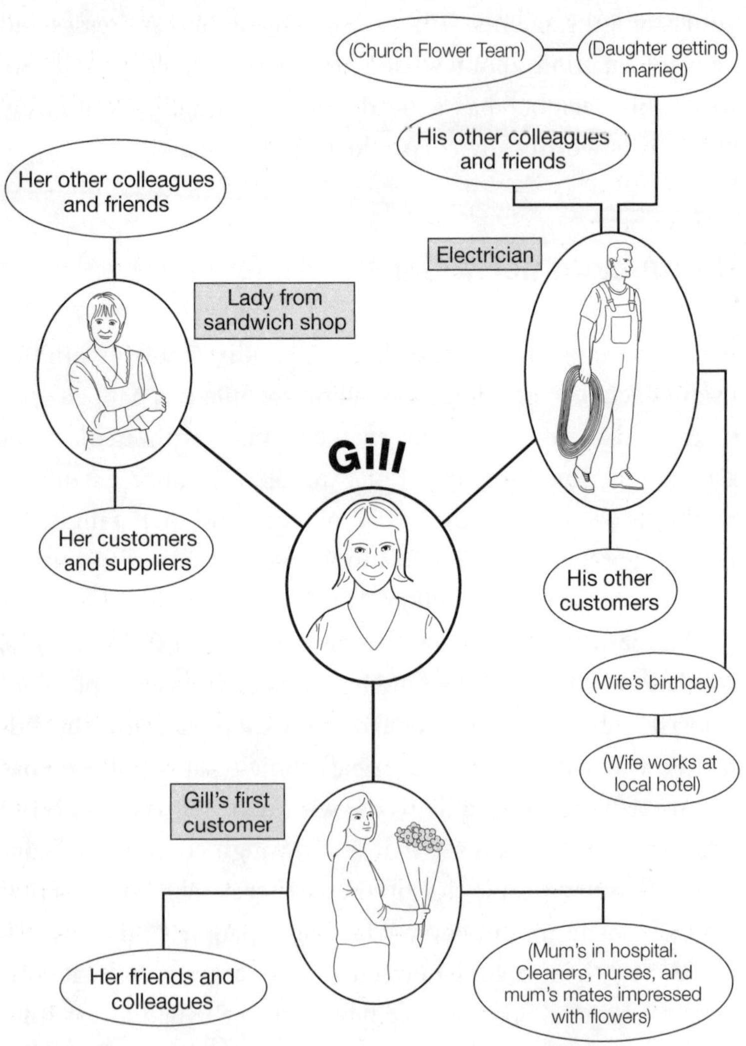

Gill's wide network after only one week in business arises from three contacts: her electrician, the lady from the sandwich shop next door and her first customer.

As you read this book we hope that you will be actively seeking out people with whom you would like to connect and purposefully nurturing those relationships. You may do this in an 'informal' way by becoming more careful, focused and skilled about the way that you interact with people you already know or will meet in your everyday life. For example, if Gill the florist wants to establish more contacts, she could invite the local business community into her shop for an opening celebration or she could attend a church event and ask to be introduced to the flower arrangers. Once she had built relationships with these people she could then ask them for other contacts who might like to know about her new shop and set about building relationships with these people too.

Networking organisations

Additionally, Gill (like you!) could also make use of one of the growing numbers of special networking organisations or events that are specifically aimed at helping people widen their circle of connections. For example, she could join her local Chamber of Commerce, the local club of an on-line business or social network or her local Women in Management or Women in Business group. (You will find more suggestions in chapter 14 of our Wise Owl Know-how section.)

In the last few years, the expanding world of the internet has opened new opportunities for strategic networking: from email to discussion forums and instant messaging. Gill could create her own website or add her profile to the websites of local trading associations to make herself visible to a wider community. (You will find much more on this in chapter 10 of our Buzzy Bee Skills section.)

Creating a networking tree

Last year, a client sent us a wonderfully creative picture of his web of contacts drawn as a tree, which he called '101 Cappuccinos'. Mark had taken voluntary redundancy from his job and we advised him that his best hope of finding a new post was through networking. Mark took some convincing at first but then became a big advocate of networking and did the illustration to help encourage others. His tree illustrated the network he built, which eventually produced contacts that gave him the job he enjoys today. The names on the trunk of the tree were contacts that Mark already had. The others were contacts he made when he actively and strategically started to network. The ringed names were those that offered Mark opportunities. These were outside Mark's immediate circle.

Why not try drawing a simple diagram or tree, as in the example on page 19, to illustrate some of your own contacts right now? Start with some of your own key personal contacts and then add branches for their friends and colleagues, and then the contacts all these people have and so on. We hope that you will be adding more and more contacts to your diagram or tree as you work through this book and begin networking more intensively.

What real confidence is (and what it isn't)

In our experience, we find that many people also have misguided ideas about confidence in relation to networking. They think that the most confident networkers are the big talkers and charismatic leaders and innovators. It is a common assumption that they are the people you would see chat-

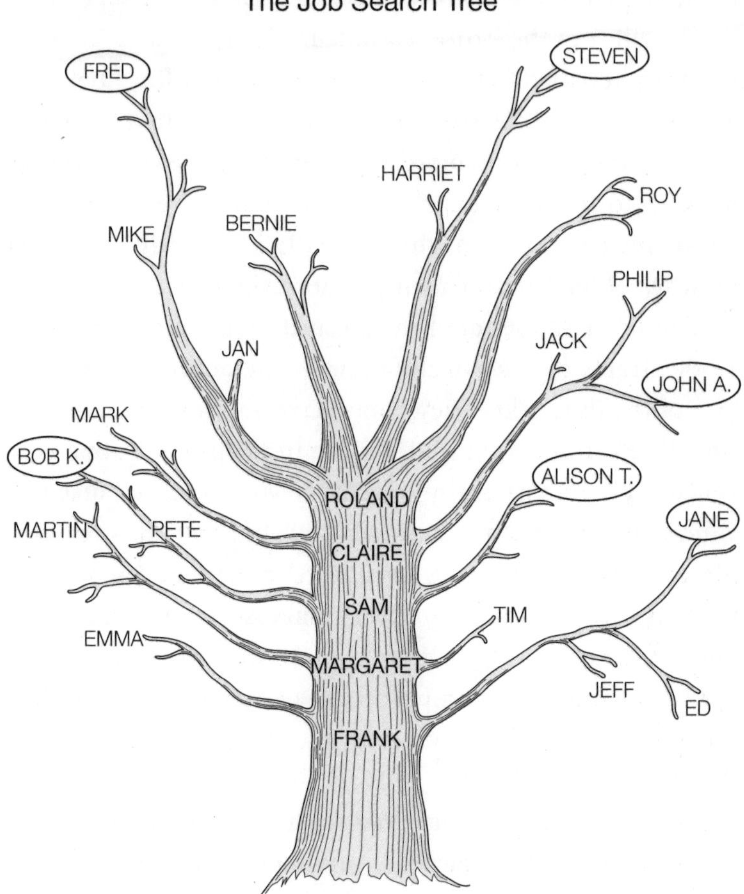

Networking tree – inspired by Mark Pyman's '101 cappuccinos'. (Circled names produced job opportunities.)

ting animatedly to all and sundry in a room of 1,000 strangers. The truth is that highly outgoing networkers such as these could be confident, or they may not be. From our experience of having had hundreds and hundreds of confidential consultations with just such people, we know that it is likely that a fair number of the 'big talkers' in such situations will not be truly confident. Indeed, they may be inwardly terrified. They could be simply bluffing their way around the room, desperately trying to bolster up their shaky self-esteem by getting more and more people to like them or look up to them. (We are sure you would agree that this is hardly the best basis on which to build a mutually supportive network of long-term trusting relationships!)

The most self-assured people in this imaginary room of 1,000 strangers could well be those interacting in the shadows of the limelight. They could have confidently chosen to stay glued to a corner and engage in deep one-to-one conversation with a carefully selected new contact because that is how they know they network best. In contrast, such people, although they may be considered 'quiet types', would not be driven by inner fears and personal insecurity. They would know what they want to gain from networking and have the self-belief and social competence to use the strengths of their introvert personality to build the kind of relationships they need.

True self-confidence develops when you are repeatedly successful while at the same time genuinely being 'yourself' and being the kind of person you can respect. Your successes can be large or small and your style of operating can be highly conspicuous or not. It can also involve great numbers of people or just a very few.

But having said how different confident people can be, there are some characteristics that they do share. Inwardly, they feel at ease with themselves and take pride in who they are and how they act – in spite of knowing they are not perfect. They know what they want and what they are capable of achieving and believe they will meet with success.

Externally, confident people radiate positive energy. They appear calm, in control and approachable and they communicate clearly and openly. They also directly ask for what they want and will unhesitatingly and effectively both promote and defend themselves whenever they choose to do so.

We are sure that you have felt and acted like 'a confident person' at least once in your life. This quick exercise will remind you how it felt. Read the instructions through and then close your eyes to do the visualisation.

- Think of a time in your life when you faced a challenge that you knew you could meet and, indeed, you did. This could be at school, work or in your personal life. It doesn't have to be a major one, but just one that you are proud of having risen to well. Relive it in your mind for a moment or two.
- Imagine now that you have been asked to face a very similar challenge.
- Visualise yourself talking to a group of unknown people and calmly convincing them of your proven ability to meet their demands.
- While continuing to watch yourself confidently talking about this challenge, notice the feeling that you are experiencing.

That feeling that you have just recreated is inner confidence and some of the behaviours you saw yourself using were self-presentation and assertive communication, which are two of the key social skills that characterise outer confidence. When a person is consistently both inwardly and outwardly confident, we would describe them as a super-confident person. That is your goal!

Some people are lucky enough to have acquired some of the key ingredients of super-confidence quite 'naturally' on their passage through life. But, there are others who do understand how difficult being a confident networker can be. The shy business tycoon and self-promoter par excellence Richard Branson is a famous example. He has had to learn, as have thousands of others we know, how to be outwardly confident. Others have had struggles with their inner confidence and problems of self-belief.

So remember, becoming confident enough to network well may be harder for some than others, but it is never impossible for anyone – including you! Read on to find out how much you have to gain from becoming a super-successful networker.

The benefits of effective networking

We firmly believe that becoming a more effective networker will make a big difference to your working life. That's why we wrote this book! If you tick any of the Yes boxes for any of the following questions you need to be a confident networker. If you aren't, you will dramatically reduce your chances of having the working life you want. We hope that you will be further inspired and convinced by reading what some of the leading voices in the world of career development and business have to say on the subject.

Answer Yes or No to the following questions by ticking the appropriate boxes:

Do you want to change the direction of your career? **Yes** ☐ **No** ☐

'The networks we rely on in a stable job are rarely the ones that lead us to something new and different . . . it is important to conduct our "role rehearsals" for our new working identity outside our usual circles because the old audience tends to narrowly typecast us.'

Herminia Ibarra, *Professor of Organisational Behaviour at INSEAD and author of* Working Identity

After reading Herminia's book a client of ours started to network. Previously he had been a very successful IT director but as a result of meeting new people his eyes were opened to different aspects of himself and new possibilities. He is now enjoying life as a school teacher.

Are you looking for a new job? **Yes** ☐ **No** ☐

'Across all industries and age groups, 66% of professionals in transition secured re-employment through networking.'

Career Choices of People in Transition – DBM Report 2003

And we know that these findings are already out of date. Fewer and fewer jobs are being advertised and employers are relying more and more heavily on networking. This is not just to save money; they find that word of mouth referral is a more effective way of recruiting.

Are you keen to be promoted? **Yes** ☐ **No** ☐

'What distinguished high performers were larger and more diversified personal networks than those of average

performers. This is consistent with other research findings, in which more diversified networks are associated with early promotion, career mobility, and managerial effectiveness.'

Rob Cross and Andrew Parker, *The Hidden Power of Social Networks (HBS Press 2004)*

Having access to a wide range of contacts beyond your immediate work circle is essential in a world that is becoming increasingly interdependent. It is now hard to be successful without a diverse network to amplify your own experience, skills and knowledge.

Do you want to reach the very top? **Yes** ☐ **No** ☐

'Leaders who can't network can't lead effectively. I am always struck by the fact that most important business decisions have been made before the meeting by people talking and linking in with others who share their view.'

Derek Wood – *London Centre for Leadership*

We regularly see and hear these kinds of decisions being made at social networking events!

Are you seeking new ways to expand your customer base? **Yes** ☐ **No** ☐

'The best prospect is the client who has already dealt with you. The second best is the one referred to you by a client who has dealt with you previously. The third best is the one referred to you by another trusted professional or friend.'

Marilyn Jennings, *author of* Championship Selling

As we said earlier, networking isn't a direct form of selling but it is an excellent tool for raising awareness of your products or services and establishing trust.

Do you want to set up a new business or charitable project? **Yes** ☐ **No** ☐

> *'For a start-up or small business, networking can provide a lifeline of support and business generation through benefits such as benchmarking; comparing and developing ideas; knowledge of best practice; staff exchanges; joint skills development to save costs; raising your business profile; generating business contacts and establishing overseas partnerships.'*
>
> Department of Trade and Industry (DTI) – *Business Link introduction to services*

And we know that it works. A recent business initiative of one of our clients is a great example of the success we regularly witness. Kevin, owner of a new logistics business, found that 13 of his 16 major client assignments came from his networking contacts. Similarly, we have seen many charity fundraisers successfully tout for support over a glass of Chardonnay!

Are you searching for investors? **Yes** ☐ **No** ☐

> *'Having recently entered into the world of venture capital, I have been struck by the considerable extent to which industry relies on networking.'*
>
> David Gilbert *is the former chief operating officer of Dixons Stores Group and managing director of Waterstone's Booksellers. As well as pursuing his venture capital interests, he acts as an adviser to the Arts Council.*

Here is an inspiring example we saw reported just today on the net: 'Oxfordshire Investment Opportunity Network raised £12 million for more than 40 innovative ventures over the last 3 years.'

Are you looking for partners with whom to forge strategic alliances? **Yes** ☐ **No** ☐

> *'Effective networking at both the personal and business to business (B2B) level is a critical competency for today's leading business executives. It allows them to build adaptable and flexible communication/influence structures which are resilient to change and valuable sources of innovation through diversity.'*
>
> Mike Nevin, *founding chairman of the Association of Strategic Alliance Professionals (Europe) Ltd*

When we decided to look for people to partner up with us to build a new Confident Networking business, our first thought was to explore the potential of both our networks. Through contacts of our contacts we found interested people within days.

Do you need to insure your career against a 'rainy day'? **Yes** ☐ **No** ☐

> *'Networking is income insurance. It is also employability insurance and I believe emotional health insurance and spiritual insurance ... you pay your health insurance premiums every month that you aren't sick. Networking is no different: you pay your premiums by making your 1,000 meetings.'*
>
> Thomas Power, *chairman of Ecademy business network*

Networking is one of the most important means by which you can take responsibility for your own career. It is very gratifying for us when ex-clients who have once been through a career shock let us know they are not sitting on their laurels ever again and are still networking in earnest.

We hope you ticked a few of the 'Yes' boxes and are now also inspired to work hard at becoming an energetic, super-confident networker. We will now move on to show you how you can be as inwardly confident as Cool Cat, as outwardly confident as Buzzy Bee and as knowledgeable as Wise Owl.

PART ONE

•

Cool Cat Qualities

In this section we will show you how to build and maintain your inner confidence. You will be working on developing the six key personal qualities that Confident Networkers commonly share. Just like our Cool Cat, they don't doubt their right to be noticed and respected because they like and value themselves. They have a great sense of personal balance, which gives them the poise to be able to assess opportunities calmly and pounce when they need to seize the moment. They also have the courage to hunt for what they need while ensuring they still have plenty of time to lounge luxuriously and recover their personal poise and appeal after a setback. Finally, they are also sensitive to others' needs and will even generously share their favourite cushion.

2

Sound self-belief

SELF-BELIEF IS THE HEART OF inner confidence. It's the psychological quality that pumps the very essence of life energy into us. Without it, our primitive urge to survive and thrive is weaker. If you network while your self-belief is shaky, you could be undermining the potential of all your strengths, skills and achievements, for the following reasons.

Firstly, you will play too safe. You will probably narrow your field of vision to people you already know. Or, to avoid getting rejected, you could stick to talking to the small minority who are so nice that they wouldn't give a brush-off to a fly sitting on their nose.

Secondly, you will almost certainly sell yourself short. You may hold back on sharing some of your strengths and achievements because you have lost faith in your ability to live up to these past standards. Or, you may do so because you fear you will be judged as overly arrogant.

Even if you do not consciously sell yourself short, your subconscious may step in and do the job for you. When our self-belief is low, we can forget some of our achievements. This is because our brains work in such a way that they automatically retrieve information from our memories which harmonises with our current emotional state. When Stuart was made redundant a few years back, the first CV he produced was appalling! Luckily, we looked it over between us before sending it out. We were shocked to see how, at this time of stress and low self-esteem, he of all people (who normally maintained well-above average confidence) had simply forgotten so many of his strengths and achievements.

Thirdly, low self-belief can also affect the social skills of outer confidence, which you will be working on in the Buzzy Bee Skills section. You will see then how crucial these skills are for interacting with people and building good relationships. The skill of listening is an example and the one that is perhaps most important in face-to-face networking. Ironically, people with low self-confidence often rank this one as their top strength. And indeed it may be – but not when their self-belief is low. In this state, they will often let themselves be 'cornered' for overly long periods by people declaiming on pet subjects or baring their souls. Being a passive aural receptacle for verbal dumping is not the same as being a great listener. The kind of listening that networking demands requires full-on concentration and low self-belief makes minds wander, especially when you are bored. You can drift into worrying about what you are going to say or how you look or whether they would like you if they really knew you.

Fourthly, low self-belief can affect your ability to process written information correctly. Gael remembers that when she first started doing training courses in the business world, the only words on the feedback forms that leapt off the page were the negative ones. She walked away from every course thinking that it was her last and was genuinely surprised whenever she was asked back to do more work. This kind of negative selective reading can be a make-or-break factor when networking electronically using emails and forums on websites. For example, a client of Stuart's recently identified someone in his network that he wanted to meet. He was dejected by her response to his email, which read: 'Thanks for making contact. Before we meet, I'd appreciate if you would let me know more about your specific experiences in this area.' Because the client's self-belief was at such a low ebb, he immediately viewed this as a rejection. The reality was, as Stuart assured him, that it was a very positive signal. He knew that this particular individual usually takes 3 months to respond to most requests!

Fifthly, low self-belief makes it much more difficult to 'Seize the moment'. In a fast-paced world we often have only fleeting moments to make a connection. If you waste time sweating about whether or not an interesting new lead or famous VIP will want to talk to you, almost certainly a cooler cat will seize your opportunity.

Finally, although low self-belief is an internal experience, it has a nasty habit of manifesting itself externally. This is what happened to Fiona, an account manager we know.

CASE STUDY

During my appraisal last month, it became obvious that my job might be at risk. I knew that I hadn't reached my target, so I was dreading it anyway, but I didn't expect it to be quite as bad. He basically told me that I hadn't got what it takes to make a good impact on customers. Looking back, I think a lot of what he said wasn't fair but I was so stunned at the time that I didn't defend myself. I just left that room determined to find another job before he got in there first with an official warning.

I immediately revved myself up into a positive mood, re-jigged my CV and set about job hunting. I have been to four networking events already in the past two weeks. The first couple were OK, but the last two were dreadful. I almost had a full-blown panic attack during the last one. I'm losing my confidence fast. I can't stop myself thinking that if I have made such a mess of this job, maybe I'll never do better in any other. I could hear myself giving my positive spiel and it sounded OK but I felt such a phoney – there was no way I could concentrate on listening to anyone else. I don't remember a single name of anyone I met at those last two events, so what's the point?'

Sadly, Fiona was right. Experienced networkers can see through phoney behaviour. And they won't like it. This is because networking is about building relationships of trust and you can't do that unless people are genuine. So there was little point in Fiona networking until she had recovered from that knock to her self-esteem. If she had taken some time out to recover emotionally and look objectively at what had happened and her real position (as she did with us later after losing her job), she could have set about networking with true, rather than fake, self-belief. Don't listen to those who say 'Fake it until you make it' when referring to self-belief.

How do you develop your self-belief?

Unlike many of the other components of self-confidence we shall be looking at later, the vast majority of us once had very good self-belief. New-born babies don't doubt their right to be noticed, liked and have their needs met. They exercise this right first by howling for attention and then through seductive smiling (which they soon learn is far more effective). Unfortunately, once past infancy, most people's self-belief takes a rocky path. Life being life, it is knocked about by failures, criticism, rejection, identity crises and comparisons. These experiences make us question whether we are entitled to use either howls or smiles to get what we need and want. Such doubts are only temporary for most people but for others they can become habitual responses. This is because they have not learned how to regularly reinforce and repair their self-belief.

There are two main ways we can learn this habit. The first is by modelling a good example. People who are lucky enough to have confident parents or parent figures do this effortlessly and unconsciously. These are the people who tend to take their self-belief for granted and would never let self-doubt hold them back.

The second way is to make a conscious effort to learn and develop the self-nurturing habits that strengthen self-belief. If you missed out on the first method, then you can go for the second right now! These tips will show you how. Why fake it when you can have the real Cool Cat thing?

Tips to help build sound self-belief

 *Stay updated on who you are today*

Leopards may not change their spots, but human beings do – thank goodness. Most people would not like to be the same as they were 20 years ago. Of course, you still have your genetic pre-dispositions and your core characteristics, which will always be with you, but you will also develop new parts of your personality as you progress through life. Everyone who lives in the real world does.

This is why self-assessment has to be a continuous process. If you believe in a self that no longer exists you will set yourself up for networking failures. You may select people that are wrong 'matches' for the new you. You could also be perceived as inauthentic because you say you are one kind of person when people can clearly see that you are not. And finally, you could disappoint yourself by going for goals that are irrelevant to your current needs.

So set aside a ten-minute period for honest self-reflection each day. Jot down in a special journal the confidence challenges you have had that day and how you fared and felt when doing them. You will enjoy looking back and seeing how you have changed. For example, you may notice that a few months back you were panicking about having to start conversations with strangers at lunch and now doing that feels so easy and makes lunch breaks so much more interesting.

But self-reflection is not enough. You must also ask regularly for honest feedback from a range of other people as well. Until your self-belief gets stronger your brain will continue to highlight your faults and mistakes, so you may be the last person to notice how you have changed for the better. Clients who do this regularly report having pleasant surprises such as being told that they are making much more impact in meetings. (You will find advice on asking for feedback on yourself in chapter 12 of Buzzy Bee Skills, page 209.)

Keep focused on your appeal to others

As a good networker your main focus should not be on what you want or need to sell. It should be on what others might need from you. You must display and highlight what you have on offer in a way that is most likely to make it relevant and appealing to the other person. When you can focus on your appeal to others you may be in for some more pleasant surprises, but when your confidence is low, you will probably undervalue what you have to offer others.

Try the unique appeal points (UAP) exercise below to help you clarify your strengths in relation to the potential needs of others. UAPs are our variation on the well-known acronym USPs (unique selling points). UAPs highlight the differences between the kind of networking we advocate and selling. This exercise will ask you to evaluate your strengths in relation to your appeal. The four key areas of strengths to analyse are as follows:

1. **Innate aptitudes:** those enduring, personality-defining core qualities that are likely to predetermine major areas of contribution in your career (e.g. extrovert, analytical and introspective).
2. **Developed character strengths:** those strengths you've developed as a result of your life experiences (e.g. patience, resourcefulness and consistency).
3. **Technical skills:** those learned competencies that you can legitimately claim as areas of special expertise. Don't overstate these, as credibility is quickly lost (e.g. language 'fluency'). Do you have ready examples or proof of these skills (e.g. PRINCE2 Accreditation, Quality Assessment, and Accountancy)?

4. **People skills:** these skills are self-explanatory and critical to networking (e.g. responsiveness, insight, co-operation).

Read our completed example below and then try the exercise for yourself. We suggest you include at least three items per category. There is a blank UAP form for you to use in Appendix 3 (pages 274–5).

UAP completed example

1. Innate aptitudes	Appeal factor	Potentially interested parties
Creative and innovative	Comes up with new solutions for intransigent problems	Companies with declining markets. Career advice and coaching agencies; people role-bound by their job description
Analytical and logical	Determines root cause of problems and plans cautiously in face of risk	Organisations with governance; quality control issues; people who are fantasy-bound and lacking pragmatic direction
'Big picture' thinker	Maintains focus on vision	De-motivated teams, especially after major changes/reorganisation; nit-pickers and detail junkies

2. Developed character strengths	**Appeal factor**	**Potentially interested parties**
Persistence and drive	Can take on long-term projects with delayed gratification	General management. Long- term research projects (e.g. pharmaceutical). Novice entrepreneurs and small business start-ups
Integrity and honesty	What you see is what you get; can be trusted to deliver on promises	Roles with significant responsibility for others. Corporate governance
Down-to-earth, pragmatic	Practical approach, focus on reality	Companies with poor track record of successful implementations. Over-impulsive people

3. Technical expertise	**Appeal factor**	**Potentially interested parties**
Information Technology (IT)	Resolve computer/ software/communication problems	Individuals or organisations looking to improve efficiency
Language competence	Improved communication across cultures and geographies	Global, multi-national operations. Post trans-national merger situations
Project management skills	Convert good ideas into workable plans and tangible results	Previously successful companies losing market share. Logistics, supply chain management roles

4. People skills	Appeal factor	Potentially interested parties
Sensitivity and empathy	Rapid, accurate understanding of client/staff needs	Client facing consultancies. Sales, training, HR. Health services
Interpersonal communication skills	Getting messages across quickly and accurately	Roles involving presenting and persuading, e.g. sales, marketing, training and change management
Helpfulness	Team player; customer liaison	Customer service. People development

 *Create opportunities to share your UAPs*

Confident Networkers seize fleeting opportunities that others may not ever even notice. If you were standing in an airport queue and spotted that the man next to you was reading an article on a topic that was of great interest to you, would you try, politely, to initiate a conversation? Let's imagine you would, and that during your five minutes of small talk, it emerges that this man works for a company that has just the kind of opportunities you are looking for. Unfortunately, you have also learned that he has a different destination from you. How well would you use the five minutes you have left of this lucky break? Would your new contact board his plane, knowing about your interest and with an accurate impression of what you as an individual might be able to offer?

If not, you may have lost an invaluable contact simply because you didn't have sound enough belief in your own UAPs. A good networker is able to accurately convey their key appealing assets to a new contact in one minute. That may sound like a tall order but it is not as impossible as it sounds. It takes preparation and practice. In chapter 8 in the Buzzy Bee Skills section, we will show you how to take advantage of many fleeting opportunities to make interesting new connections.

 *Use your strengths to control your weaknesses*

Many people mistakenly think that self-belief can be improved by forcing yourself not to think of your weaknesses. We find that doing this can create a forbiddingly perfect front, not to mention self-delusion. Truly confident people accept themselves warts and all. They also trust that others will too. The main reason they are able to do both is that they have learned to use their strengths to help them stay in control of their weaknesses.

Some common networking 'weaknesses' are simply bad habits rather than innate personality traits. Admittedly some of these can be very entrenched if they were established at an early age and can feel irreversible. But they rarely are, as Mary's story illustrates:

CASE STUDY

Mary was well aware of her tendency to interrupt others, especially when people were struggling to express themselves. Finishing off others' sentences is an irritating auto-response that she thinks she picked up from her father. She hates hearing herself doing this, especially as she knew how much her father's impatience had annoyed her as a child. But she has now learned to use her empathy (one of her greatest strengths) to control this tendency. In the early stages of a conversation, she has trained herself to consider what the other person may be feeling. If the answer is something like 'anxious', this is her signal to take a couple of slightly deeper breaths to ensure she is more relaxed and can be the caring adult she is today.

Of course the people who are struggling to express themselves and irritating Mary could do something to control their weaknesses as well! Have a look at our examples below.

Examples of strengths used to control weaknesses

Strengths	Weakness correction
Persistence	apply it to breaking bad conversational habits by preparing what you want to say and then editing and practising your 'script' over and over again until it is punchy and precise
Honesty	remind yourself how much you value this quality to motivate you to be assertive and beat the habit of biting your tongue when someone unfairly criticises or shows disrespect
Courage	recall a time when you used your courage and feel its power to stop you 'chickening out' of striking up a conversation with someone you know who is highly successful
Analytical	use the power of your logical reasoning to analyse the true extent of the damage you did when dwelling on a mistake such as getting someone's name wrong

Strengths	**Weakness correction**
Humour	use it to help lighten the tone of a conversation you have made heavy by talking too earnestly on a serious topic while everyone else was engaged in small talk
Humility	recall the face of a role model who helped build this quality in you (e.g. a grandparent, teacher or saint) when you are rationalising away your need for support

There are of course many other types of weaknesses that may be undermining your confidence. Two very different kinds would be, for example, a physical disability such as deafness or a socially induced one such as being out of a job. You can still apply the same strategy. When you feel depressed about it, refocus your attention on finding an aspect of your character, or one of your skills, that can help you manage the weakness better. For example, use your courage to motivate you to be more assertive and ask for more help. Your self-belief will be strengthened immediately.

 *Make a contingency plan for recovering from personal knocks*

Your self-belief will be considerably strengthened if you know that you will be able to recover your cool if you are not as successful as you had hoped. As a Confident Networker we hope that you will be meeting many, many new people. There are no guarantees that all these people will treat you with respect or be at all interested in what you have to offer. In fact, let us be bold and declare the opposite to be true! You are certain to meet with some rudeness and rejections.

But don't panic; the plan we outline below will ensure you make a full emotional recovery. You can use it as a contingency plan whenever you think you risk being emotionally hurt (e.g. going to a big event where there will be many busy, popular and important people that you might want to approach). Pop a copy into your briefcase or handheld-computer as well. You will then have it at hand as a guide to help you with your emotional recovery should you receive an unexpected knock.

It is important not to skip any of the steps and you must do them in the order we suggest. Try it and see what a difference it makes. Each step is based on the 'normal' self-healing behaviour that people with high self-esteem engage in without being aware that they are doing anything special. We consider it to be very special. Since we identified this positive healing process and used it to design strategies such as the plan below, it has made an unbelievable difference to thousands of people's lives including our own. We are so sure that using it repeatedly will bolster your self-belief that we were even tempted to issue a guarantee!

Contingency plan for recovering from personal knocks

STEP 1: Calm your pulse

Here are some suggestions and examples for you to try:

- retreat to somewhere private (the loo would do!) and engage in some controlled breathing and stretching exercises
- visualise a peaceful place or the face of someone you love
- go for a quiet walk around the block
- listen to a calming CD or hum a peaceful and rhythmic melody

STEP 2: Boost your self-esteem

- give (or plan to give) yourself a treat such as a break and some favourite food or buy yourself a small luxury
- look at some reminders of past achievements (this is easier to do if you have a selection of these, such as testimonials, certificates and photos, stored in a special box or file on your computer)
- immerse yourself in an activity that you enjoy and will guarantee a satisfying result
- ring a friend whom you know will love to hear from you
- do a colleague, friend or neighbour a favour
- make a donation of time or money to a charity
- look through your networking contacts and find two people who might benefit from being introduced to each other

STEP 3: Analyse the facts

- summarise what exactly happened using objective, third-person language, free of superlatives, generalisations and exaggerations
- talk it through with an empathic but also level-headed colleague, boss or mentor

STEP 4: Reflect on your learning

- note what the experience has helped you learn about yourself, other people, communication, the type of event or networking in general

STEP 5: Make one or more resolutions

- script and rehearse an assertive response to use at your next meeting (see Buzzy Bee Skills, chapter 12, pages 206–9)
- write a letter of complaint

- apologise or make recompense
- enlist on a training course to improve a skill (see Wise Owl Know-how, chapter 18, pages 259–60)
- try an alternative networking scenario (see Wise Owl Know-how, chapter 14, pages 231–4).

3

Incorruptible integrity

INTEGRITY IS VITALLY IMPORTANT IN networking. You can only have self-respect if you believe that you are someone who can be trusted to behave with integrity.

Similarly, mutual respect is an essential component of a network. It can only exist if the members believe they can rely on the integrity of its members. When this kind of trust is established the members have confidence in the network. It becomes the kind of place where they can truly be themselves, share ideas, recommend contacts, exchange valuable information and start new working relationships and alliances.

You have probably already realised the importance of integrity to self-confidence, but perhaps until now you haven't ever considered just how much of an issue it is in networking too. So let's consider this aspect in some more detail.

Like most people, there must have been many times in your life when you have spontaneously offered up 'proof' of someone's integrity while recommending them. You may remember having said something like: 'In the five years that we have been doing business together she has always been true to her word, so I am sure she will not let you down.' Alternatively, perhaps when providing a testimonial based on experience, you may have included a 'get-out' remark such as: 'Last week I met someone who might be able to help you. He seemed the trustworthy kind to me, though I have to say I haven't actually put him to the test myself.'

At some instinctive level, we all know the power of a 'bad apple' to contaminate the integrity of others. So we naturally build in these kinds of protective clauses to protect our own reputation.

Integrity and the strong network

As we said earlier, integrity is crucial in networking because it feeds trust. In fact we believe that the strength of a network is directly related to the perceived level of integrity of its members. Ironically, this fact can be graphically illustrated by looking at the role of integrity within evil networks.

Every undercover cop and agent (and gangster!) knows the surest way to destroy the strength of a criminal network is to corrupt the sense of mutual trust. The members of evil networks may be as dishonest, unreliable and disloyal as the devil himself outside the network, but never within it. The Godfather films demonstrated the importance of this key networking 'law': the issue of integrity was a central theme and the director played mercilessly with our emotional dilemmas around it. While being terrified and horrified by the Mafia brutality, we found ourselves condoning the violent punishments that were meted out to the traitors. Because we had been so emotionally drawn into the close 'family' network, we felt their deep pain and 'justified' anger when a fellow member abused the mutual trust.

You may already have noticed that people who lead networks on both sides of the moral fence often use the analogy of 'family'. (This metaphor is often used to describe church networks as well as gangs.) The image of a family has the power to conjure up a sense of trust. Even if our personal experience of family was not good, most of us subconsciously associate 'family' with mutual moral commitment. When an abuse of trust takes place within a family, we don't just 'judge' it to be wrong with our conscious minds. We are also instinctively filled with feelings of horror and anger. This is because our primitive subconscious mind has sensed our 'survival' has been threatened. Evolution demands that families stay morally bonded together. When they are, they are more motivated to care for their weaker members and fight together when faced with external threats. Mistrust weakens the moral ties and so threatens the family's stability and strength.

In a strong business network, an abuse of mutual trust will be met with similar feelings of horror. Its connections also grow from similar shared needs such as mutual caring and economic interdependence. When someone appears to act without integrity, deep feelings of disgust and fear are automatically generated. The behaviour feels just as traitorous as it does in a family betrayal, even if rational minds know it is in a different moral league (The bottom line – 'business is business' argument).

This is why it is so important to be aware of the moral codes of each network that you join. This is as true for the more formal kinds such as a club or business specifically set up to facilitate networking or the informal ones such the neighbourhood community that our florist Gill tapped into. There are some obvious 'sins' that most networks of any description share in condemning:

- taking advantage of someone's lack of confidence or inarticulacy to dominate a conversation or make fun of them behind their back
- requesting a meeting for information gathering, but then going for the 'hard sell'
- gossiping about others behind their back
- abusing someone's good nature by letting them do all the clearing up after your meetings
- sneaking in the back door so as to avoid paying the entrance fee to a talk
- leaving just in time to avoid paying for the next round of drinks.

Each and every one of these kinds of practices damages the trust within the whole network and undermines its potential to help everyone. Here is a true story that illustrates this fact:

CASE STUDY

Jane was starting a new consultancy and wanted help with marketing her services to government departments. She asked a well-connected network contact, Brian, for help with an introduction to someone involved in government contracts so that she could learn about purchasing procedures for suppliers. Brian provided a well-placed contact, Roger. Unfortunately, on meeting Roger, Jane was very pushy and tried to force him to commit to placing an order for her services. Roger remained polite (mindful of his commitment to his relationship with Brian), but resisted the efforts of Jane to place an order. When, however, he next met Brian, he mentioned Jane's pushiness, for which Brian apologised and made a mental note never to recommend Jane again. This incident shook Brian's confidence in the network as a whole.

Consider for a moment the following weblog, posted today on an electronic business network:

I have just noticed that one of our members is involved with a person, who has a history of fabricating the truth and not delivering on promises.

I do not know how involved this person is, since I do not want to affect a business relationship. However, I now feel I cannot do business with the first person because of the second. It goes deeper because, if this second person is going to become heavily involved with this network in a big way, I will leave.

Your views and suggestions, please?

Many thanks.

As a small exercise for your integrity, think about how you would have responded to this person's appeal.

Would you, for example, have said that you understand his concern or would you have said that he was becoming over-emotional and over-suspicious? Do you think he should be advised to just wait until he sees evidence of malpractice in his dealings with the second person? Would you turn down a good business opportunity with the latter because he had associations with a person you knew lacked integrity? Would you question the organisation that welcomed such a person into its fold?

We are fairly sure this exercise would have raised uncomfortable feelings for you. We say this because, in our experience, people who do not have a lot of self-confidence continually worry, and indeed over-worry, about their integrity. When speaking confidentially to us, they commonly admit to these kinds of concerns:

> *'I tend to panic and might be unreliable because I might decide not to turn up at the last minute.'*
>
> *'When I was describing my past achievements, it didn't feel honest because I kept thinking about how many failures I had as well.'*
>
> *'I haven't done anything with that contact you gave me because I couldn't decide whether I should come clean about having been made redundant or not.'*
>
> *'I have been avoiding the meetings because I don't want to bump into Cecilia. I know you think I am a coward but I don't know how to tell her that I have placed my business with another supplier.'*

Of course it is natural for all of us with a conscience to sometimes query our own integrity – after all, we were born fallible humans and not saints. Problems however arise when the extent of that worry incapacitates us by undermining our self-confidence. Self-respect and self-trust are essential elements of inner confidence and we can only have both if we believe that our own integrity is good enough most of the time. This is our aim in giving you these tips. So don't expect a halo even if you follow them to the letter. But we do hope that your internal moral fibre and self-respect will be strengthened

Tips to help you maintain incorruptible integrity

Create your own code of networking ethics

This will give you a standard by which to monitor your integrity. Many networking organisations have established codes of ethics for themselves but, good as they often are, usually these are too long to be a quick reference guide. As a working tool, for the purposes of keeping your confidence high, all you need is a list of six to eight values that can be easily committed to memory. Your list might include obvious qualities such as honesty; respect and reliability, but do try also to include words that have personal meaning for you.

First, you could research some other networking codes. Start by looking at those of the organisations to which you belong. We have included, as an example, Ecademy's code to start you thinking. It was recently revised after some lively consultation with the members. We think it is excellent, but you may disagree. That is fine – as long as you are clear about what you would replace it with. The second example is a simple personal code.

Examples of networking codes of ethics

EXAMPLE 1: Ecademy's code

1. Members should be polite and courteous in their written tone. Sadly, without the face to face advantages of our offline events, body language cannot be read and therefore sarcasm and innuendo can be misinterpreted and cause offence.

2. Honesty is critical and we will not tolerate misrepresentation of names and services. Don't be afraid to reveal the real you as well as the business you; people like to do business with people.

3. Kindness towards your fellow member is encouraged. Being willing to help, listen, advise and pass referrals is a core principle at Ecademy. Help one another by giving not taking and never ask for something in return.

4. Being open-minded to the opinions of others will help you get more from Ecademy. Many opinions are shared here; being oversensitive or closed-minded will restrict your opportunity to learn. Remember, constructive criticism can be very valuable.

5. Giving personal criticism or airing your views against a member must be directed carefully as a message direct to them. Public attacks on individuals are noted by members and the management team. If they occur regularly from the same individual, warnings will be issued to the offending member with the appropriate explanation of the way their behaviour has offended.

6. Treat others as you would like to be treated, a great saying, and so true here. Act with professional maturity if you join

debates and always keep focused on the topic of the debate that you are joining. They are great fun when treated with humour and courtesy.

7. Thank and acknowledge members who deserve it. If someone has been kind then add this to their Guest Book as a testimonial.

8. Welcome members from around the world into your network; they can provide you with help on business issues, cultural questions, travel, holidays, the best restaurant to visit in their city and even retrieve a teddy left on holiday (it has been known!).

EXAMPLE 2: a personal code

When networking, I will endeavour to be:

- honest
- respectful
- courageous
- generous
- open-minded
- humble.

Make sure that you keep a copy of your own simple list of guiding values highly visible to you. It does not have to be made public. You need to see it regularly until your key operating principles are firmly lodged in your subconscious mind. Once they are, you will find that they will pop up into your consciousness just when you need them. For example, let's imagine that you are stuck worrying about whether to confront someone who has let you down or have been stunned into inaction by a rude brush-off. You will find that a value from your list such as 'courage' will flash into your mind. This acts as a gentle 'push off the fence' and helps you confidently decide upon a morally justified response.

 *Write a testimonial for yourself*

This task may feel both strange and arrogant. But don't avoid it for either reason. You would do it for a friend, wouldn't you?

The testimonial doesn't need to be a great literary piece; it can be done in bullet points if you wish. It should contain at least three (but preferably more) examples of your integrity in action. The following one was written by Sean, the successful owner of a small catering business:

> *'I believe in giving customers full and honest information. My customer feedback constantly shows that this is appreciated.*
>
> *'I can be relied upon to deliver on my promises. My records demonstrate that I have met 100 per cent of this year's order deadlines.*
>
> *'As this is essentially a small family business with a cherished reputation, all new lines are checked for quality by me personally. They are tried and tested in my own home before they reach the customer.'*

Sean struggled over writing this. However, he actually admitted finding some pleasure from the even harder task of reading it aloud to others on the workshop. So when you have done yours, find a friend to listen to yours and see if you feel comfortable and confident going public with it.

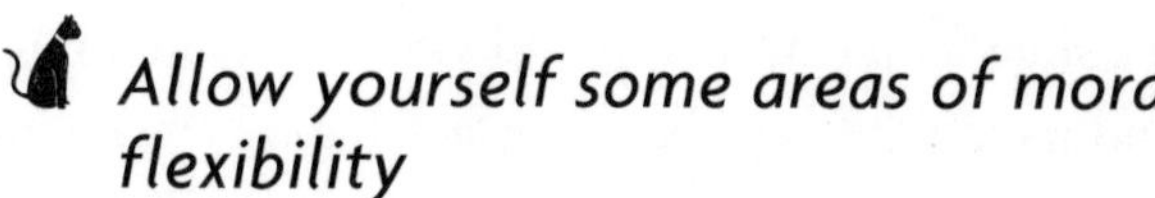

Allow yourself some areas of moral flexibility

Be prepared for common moral dilemmas. This will help you to act decisively and confidently when you come across them in real life. Imagine the kind of scenarios in which they may occur. Then ask yourself the following kinds of soul-searching questions:

- In what circumstances is it OK to tell a white lie or avoid telling the whole truth?
- Should you allow yourself to hide some facts about yourself when trying to make a good impression with an employer or business contact?
- If you meet someone whom you do not like or trust, do you need to be 100 per cent honest when you decline to work or socialise with them?

Be sure that you can justify each decision you take. For example: 'It is justified because it is unnecessary to hurt this person's feelings' or 'I need to maintain my privacy and have a right to do so.' Also, as there are always risks attached to slipping off the ethical path, be sure that you know how you will deal with each situation should you be 'found out'.

Check frequently that you are behaving authentically

You cannot maintain strong inner confidence unless you are truly being yourself most of the time. Of course, there are occasions in networking when you may decide to act in an 'inauthentic' way. For example you may choose to bite your tongue and tone down your inquisitive side with new acquaintances from countries such as Japan or Finland where personal reticence is common. Or, you may choose to 'act' happy when you are actually feeling gutted about a personal matter because you want to protect your privacy or the other person's joy in their success or good news.

When you make this kind of conscious choice to play a role for a 'good' reason your confidence will not be undermined. However, we find that unconfident people habitually use inauthentic behaviour for the 'wrong' reasons. A common example is for people to act as though they are highly interested in someone's service simply because they have a pleasing-people habit that originated in their childhood.

Another behaviour we frequently observe is giving the impression that you are more willing and able to help someone out than you actually are. Sometimes people do this because they just don't have the assertive skills to say 'No'. But sometimes they are doing it because they slip too easily into autopilot mode when faced with someone in need. Their facial expression may look more like that of a caring mum or dad than that of a realistic business colleague.

If you act in an inauthentic way too often, people will soon distrust you and distance themselves from you. To ensure that you are authentic:

- ask yourself frequently 'Am I being myself?'
- curb overly 'nice' time-wasting behaviour by reminding yourself that it is inappropriate and dishonest

- indicate clearly when you have no need of someone's services or products and politely move the conversation on in another direction
- if you can't or don't want to help someone, briefly convey your sympathy and state that you hope they can find a solution or recommend a contact who may be able to help them
- brush up on your assertiveness skills (see Buzzy Bee Skills, chapter 12, pages 200–11).

Check your motivation before giving a contact

If you are a saint – move on, you won't need this tip. If, however, you are human, you may well sometimes sin when offering a contact. So check your motivation from time to time. Ask yourself if you are merely helping yourself to some short-term goodwill, rather than being genuine in your concern to put two people in contact with each other. It won't serve the networking needs of anyone concerned if you pass on an inappropriate name just to impress.

Similarly, it won't help anyone if you give away a contact simply because someone has 'pressurised' you into doing so. Should, for example, a pushy networker whom you have just met immediately try to extract an entry contact to an organisation you know, resist. Even if this person is someone important whom you might want to impress, giving away a contact before you have done your 'moral' duty as a good networker is short-sighted. So, firmly and repeatedly stall the request by saying that you have made it a rule for yourself not to pass on contacts until you are confident you know someone and/or their work sufficiently well. Well-intentioned people will respect this kind of personal rule and admire you for having it and sticking by it.

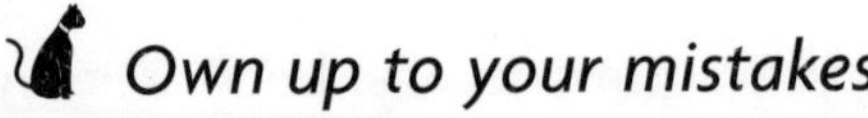

Own up to your mistakes

This may appear an obvious tip, but how often do you do it? People lacking in confidence often mistakenly think that their reputation will be damaged by being up front about mistakes. The opposite is true. It is in fact trust-building to own up to any kind of failure. The proviso to this general rule is that it should be done in a confident manner. A frank admission of guilt, accompanied whenever possible by a statement about what you have learned and how you intend to rectify it or offer recompense, is empowering for you and good for your reputation.

Be aware of when you are stepping in and out of selling mode

The line that separates the networking and selling modes may sometimes seem very faint, but nevertheless you mustn't miss it. Overstepping it can be highly counter-productive and is bad news for your integrity. However faint, it always exists. As we discussed in our introduction, networking is about establishing win/win focused relationships which might become mutually beneficial. We display rather than sell our wares. There may, of course, come a time when you want to move a relationship on, either temporarily or permanently, into a commercial mode. But, if you are keen to preserve your integrity this must be done with great care. In Buzzy Bee Skills, chapter 9, pages 151–6, we will explain a strategy to help you to make this cross-over in a professional and safe manner. For the moment, we suggest that you just concentrate on becoming more aware of when you, or other people, are stepping on to that line. Here are a couple of tell-tale signs. When moving into selling mode people tend to:

- start asking more closed questions, e.g. those beginning with When, Which, Who, How many
- find themselves physically opposite, facing the other party (the 'confrontational' business position), rather than in the more collaborative 90° position.

4

Resilient drive

NETWORKING IS NOT EASY FOR anyone at times. It's essentially a 'long slog' activity and requires a good deal of Cool Cat patience. It doesn't help that compared to many other aspects of work it has relatively undefined and distant goals. Deric and Angela's stories below represent the kind of journey that even highly motivated and dedicated networkers face.

When Deric's role as a chief operating officer in the South American division of a major oil business disappeared, he had to return to the UK and build a new network from scratch. He told Stuart that he had felt intimidated by the prospect of having to do this:

> *'... but I knew I had to persist because using job advertisements and head-hunters had been fruitless. Initially it was very difficult and I seemed to be getting nowhere. I became depressed and needed constant reminders of my*

talents and boosts to my self-esteem in order to stay on track. It wasn't until my 163rd contact that I got lucky. It directly led me into my present job which is an ideal one for me.'

Similarly, Gael was told a story by Angela, a manager of an incentive travel business. It was 18 months before networking gave her the big break. She had regularly attended meetings of several networking organisations and also given many talks at relevant conferences. Then:

'... quite unexpectedly, I found myself sitting on a plane with someone who had heard me speak two months previously. It emerged that he was currently looking at various incentive schemes for his sales force. This led to our company's biggest ever deal.'

You can never forecast where or when you will meet those key people with contacts that will make a difference. So there can never be a clear map to guide and support you along your networking path. And, moreover, having one would defeat the object of the exercise. Networking works best when we are 'following our noses' and trying out new routes that we may never even have known existed. This is why all the gurus tell you to focus on the journey and not the destination. The theory being that if the travelling is fun and interesting, you will want to continue. Much of the time this advice holds true. Networking, in our experience, does usually feel like an enjoyable adventure. The majority of people we meet are pleasant and stimulating and there are plenty of unexpected surprises and coincidences that keep our curiosity alive.

But, there are also times when you can be standing in a

crowded room and suddenly feel as though you are surrounded by alien creatures. There seems no way of breaking through into the tightly knit web of chattering circles. At other times you may feel that all you ever do is idle away time with superficial acquaintances and the only outcome is a pocket full of irrelevant business cards. On other occasions, you may feel like you are constantly being sucked dry by needy people and give out endlessly with no return. Or, if you are very unlucky, you may encounter a surfeit of people who are plain boring, downright rude or dishonest.

And (dare we mention it!), there will also, of course, be occasions when you deserve a setback. You may have been lazy or badly prepared and, as a result, lost the biggest opportunity of your lifetime.

These down-times are a difficult challenge to anyone's motivation. And it is normal to feel disheartened and annoyed. But, if your confidence was shaky before you met the 'obstacle', you may view it not so much as a temporary irritation, but a welcome excuse to quit. It might be perceived as 'proof' that networking is useless or too difficult for you.

This is why you cannot ever afford to take your motivation for granted. To help yourself withstand the exit temptations of testing times, you need to inoculate yourself with above average drive, energy and emotional resilience. Unlike the superconfident networkers, you cannot count on your autopilot to get you back on a positive track. Unless you are regularly feeding it with positive programming, in the face of a setback, it is more likely to freeze you into apathy or depression or make you take flight. The following tips will help you build your 'cool' so you can keep on prowling through the longest and darkest of nights.

Tips for building and maintaining resilient drive

Plant positive visions in your mind

Remember William Wordsworth's poem 'The Daffodils'? We guess you do as most of us were at some stage of our childhood made to learn it off by heart. But it is unlikely that your teachers would have told you that it is an excellent example of the power of positive visioning.

I wandered lonely as a cloud
That floats on high o'er vales and hills,
When all at once I saw a crowd,
A host of golden daffodils; beside the lake, beneath the trees,
Fluttering and dancing in the breeze.

... when on my couch I lie
In vacant or pensive mood,
They flash upon that inward eye
Which is the bliss of solitude;
And then my heart with pleasure fills,
And dances with the daffodils.

Nowadays many people employ expensive psychologists to teach them the same mood-enhancing trick! It has now become known in the trade as the technique of 'creative visualisation'. A past experience of pleasure or an imagined vision of future success can be used to create an energising optimistic mood. It is a favourite with modern sports coaches and many footballers admit to using it.

Creative visualisation is simple and quick to learn. Follow these steps and repeat the exercise as frequently as you can for the next few weeks until you have trained yourself in the technique and then you will be able to use it wherever and whenever you need an extra dose of positive energy:

- Release the tension from your body by doing a few stretches or clenching and slowly releasing tight muscles.
- Sit or lie in a well-supported position and close your eyes.
- Take three to five slow deep breaths, focusing on the passage of your breath in and out of your body. It sometimes helps to imagine the in breath as one colour and the out breath as another.
- Allow yourself to sink heavily into the chair, bed or floor that is supporting you and let yourself float into a deeply relaxed state.
- Use your imagination to run a mental movie of yourself being successful at whatever it is you want to achieve. This could be, for example, giving a talk, approaching an important person to introduce yourself or playing host at a lively social event.
- Re-run the movie a couple of times, each time making the colours more vibrant and sounds crystal clear and notice the positive feelings, physical sensations and the energy watching this scene triggers.

Why does such a simple trick work? In short, because planting a positive image in your subconscious brain will switch your brain into the mode whereby it will automatically generate the endorphin hormones that will give you a natural 'high'.

It is important to remember that the more relaxed you are (remember Wordsworth was lying on his couch when he wrote

'The Daffodils'), and the more vibrant the picture in your mind is, the better the result will be.

 *Convert your envy into positive learning*

Recall a few of those networkers who ooze with the confidence you lack. Next time you see them in action, observe them closely. Notice the self-assured pace they use to walk into a room; the comfortable looseness of their limbs when they talk on the phone and the well-supported posture they maintain at their desk. As they converse, listen to the lively tone of their voices; watch their expressive facial and hand movements and see the sparkle in their eyes.

Choose three of these people to be your special role models. Then, use your mind's eye to watch a ten-second 'recording' of each of them in action. For the next week, run the same three short movies in your head at a regular time each day. Establishing this kind of routine will help you to remember to do the exercise. It could be done on the train or bus on the way to work, or just before you take your morning coffee break. As you watch your role models in action, smile with pleasure (internally if you must!). Research has shown that using the smiling muscles in your face actually stimulates the production of those hormones which elevate our mood, and it has also proved that when we are happy we learn more effectively.[1]

You can also use this particular mental movie trick whenever your internal green-eyed monster starts its 'I wish I was more like …' depressing game. The more you watch your role models in your mind, the more you will automatically find yourself using their body language without having to make a conscious effort to do so.

Now, that's the kind of learning that appeals to us. No doubt it does to you too?

 *Isolate yourself from unnecessary external negative influences*

We would like to hazard a guess that you are currently overdosing on negative experiences. We say this because we have yet to meet anyone lacking confidence who doesn't. It is unlikely that you will be consciously seeking out ways to depress yourself, but you will be drawn into doing so because:

- often you feel powerless to control your external world. This means that you will not be as proactive as a highly confident person in seeking out positive paths
- your brain is automatically homing in on the negative data stored within your memory and the gloomy side of current life experiences to make a match with your basic fearful mood
- you are too 'nice'! It is unlikely that you are currently being adequately assertive. People who lack confidence are generally not the best at protecting themselves from people who discourage, disrespect or bully them. (We have some good tips for overcoming this later in Buzzy Bee Skills, chapter 12, pages 200–11.)

Until you have built up your confidence and corrected these habits, it is best to isolate yourself as much as possible from negative influences. For the next month make a conscious effort to:

- spend as little time as you can with people who don't like people! You know the ones we mean only too well. They are the relatives, friends, customers and colleagues who believe 'You can't trust anyone further than you can throw them'

- watch or listen to fewer 'bad news' stories in the media. Unless it is absolutely necessary to your job, limit yourself to a couple of updates a day and focus on the positive elements of the stories, such as the way people have rallied together to help in times of disaster or the victims who are constructively using their experience to campaign for change
- select your entertainment and culture input carefully. Take care that the upbeat TV programmes, films, music and books outnumber the blue and the tragic
- archive or throw away any reminders of disappointment, pain and failure. These could be files on unsuccessful projects or they could be letters, emails, posters, photos or mementos on display in your home or office. (Watching the shredder at work or making a bonfire of the offending material can be very motivating!)
- ensure that your virus checker is up to date and is filtering out annoying unsolicited newsletters and spam
- choose as often as you can to go to the networking events that are held in pleasant venues and do not entail depressing, tiring journeys.

By the end of the month, you should notice a change in your mood and in your behaviour. You should be feeling more positive and be automatically veering towards the smilers among the crowds.

 *Spend more time on the aspects of your work you enjoy*

This is obviously easier to do if you are self-employed or work for a company that allows you to manage your work-load. In the short term, this may mean sacrificing some financial gain or working slightly longer hours. But rest assured that the strategy will eventually pay off. You are much more likely to have a successful career if you enjoy your work. Pleasure is actually a more effective motivator than money. And, when we are enjoying ourselves we tend to perform better. Think of the many millionaires who continue working even though they no longer need the money. They continue to work for sheer pleasure and satisfaction.

Perhaps this all sounds right now like an impossible and overly idealist dream. Maybe you are in a job that you hate and are reading this book in the hope that it will help you to escape it as quickly as possible. If so, it is even more important that you take this tip on board. There has got to be at least some small aspect of your work that you do enjoy (or could enjoy). This could be the planning of a new project or your relationship with certain customers or colleagues. Spending just a little more time on these tasks would help lift your spirits and make you more emotionally resilient to the negative effects of the rest of your work. You will then have more drive and energy for the Confident Networking that will lead you to the job you really want.

 *Do regular energy audits*

Networking demands extra physical energy. Invariably, it has to be done in addition to your normal work-load. This means that you must find a way to generate more stamina. If you are tired before you even start, you will be much more vulnerable to dips in your confidence. (Who doesn't feel braver after a great night's sleep or a week's rejuvenating holiday?)

Unless you are in the league that can pay for a professional, become your own personal trainer:

- consult your doctor to find out in what range your individual optimum fitness level should be
- check the functioning of your heart and lungs regularly by giving yourself tests such as running up the stairs and walking very briskly to work. You could wear a heart monitor while doing these activities
- chart in your diary your actual level of fitness on a certain day each month. If you fall below your optimum range, take immediate action. Early action should only involve a little extra exercise, a slightly better diet or 15 minutes more sleep.

Keep a prepared checklist of self-rewards

Cool Cats never let their motivation become dependent on enticing tit-bits and strokes from others. They reward themselves. This is another good habit only super-confident networkers have developed. When we ask our clients to list the typical rewards they give themselves when they have achieved something difficult, we are almost always met with a blank look.

Do you congratulate yourself and treat yourself each time you have met a challenging goal, such as getting in touch with a high flying contact? Even more importantly, would you do this if you overcame your nerves and made the call, but didn't get an appointment? You would probably do neither. In the first instance you are likely to think the fruits of your success are enough reward and in the second, that you deserve a kick and not a pat on the back.

Research has proved that humans are more motivated by reward than punishment. But just knowing the facts like this doesn't break bad habits. They have to be killed off by good ones. So make a graded list of affordable self-rewards and place this somewhere where you will see it continually to serve as a motivational reminder.

And remember, if you want to maintain resilient drive it is more important to reward your everyday good efforts than it is to reward yourself for your major successes.

Appoint a couple of language watch-dogs

Ask for help from a couple of colleagues or friends who meet these three criteria: they are highly observant, care about you, and are positive thinkers. Their first task is to spot when you are talking in a negative, self-defeating way. Their second (until you can do this part yourself) is to suggest an alternative and positive way of phrasing what you have just said. In the therapy business this is called 'reframing' and is another simple but highly effective mind programming 'trick'. The positive language is perceived by the brain as a signal to produce endorphins in order to produce a compatible mood. Another theory claims that reframing works because it effectively 'scrambles' the pattern of the negative auto-response. As a result the cognitive brain is then triggered into rational thinking.

Here are some examples:

Reframing negative language

☹ There are going to be too many people there to have any meaningful conversation.

☺ With that many going, it will be a good opportunity to practise my new small talk openers.

☹ There's no point in ringing, I'll most likely just get an answerphone.

☺ Having to leave a message will give me a chance to make a more confident impression because I can rehearse my introduction first.

☹ I'm nervous enough about meeting new people face to face. It can only be more difficult on the internet when you can't even see who you are talking to.

☺ At least my nerves won't show when I first meet people on the internet. And I will get a chance to think through my responses before answering their questions.

Show these examples to your potential watch-dogs. They should immediately show interest and enthusiasm. Ask them if they would be prepared to monitor you for a realistic time period such as a month. (You may be lucky enough to find someone who will take on this task for life. We are still doing it for each other after 23 years!)

Should your potential watch-dogs not react enthusiastically or find the task too daunting, thank them for listening and quickly find someone else. Don't attempt to beg or persuade. It is important to have well-motivated and super-positive thinkers in this role. Trust that someone will be more than willing to help. We believe most positive thinkers would feel honoured to help in this way.

 *Think long term not short term*

Don't forget that Confident Networking is a way of life and an investment in the future. You may lose an odd battle or two but your overall strategy will eventually ensure that you are a winner.

5

Genuine generosity

RECIPROCITY IS A BASIC PRINCIPLE of networking. Harvey Mackay, author of *Dig Your Well Before You're Thirsty*, claims that in networking 'You are only as good as what you give away.' So our principle objective is to effect exchanges; to both give and receive. It is true that we may not always receive the instant we give, or receive from the person to whom we give, but we do expect that, overall, the exchange will be two-way and that it will be mutually beneficial.

In essence, therefore, networking is a business and not a charity. The irony, however, is that the more charitably we give, the more business results we are likely to receive.

Mick Cope, the author of *Personal Networking*, explains this principle in terms of the social abundance theory: 'the belief that 2 + 2 = 5, that there is enough cake for everyone and that you can give and the get will come later. … the whole ethos of networking is that it must be grounded in an abundance mentality.'

Rob Cross and Andrew Parker, authors of *The Hidden Power of Social Networks*, studied this ironic principle in action. As a result of their research, they concluded that it works because it builds benevolence-based trust: 'Giving without expecting something in return is a show of trust. In such situations, the giver takes initial action based on the belief that the receiver will respond in kind at some future point.' Interestingly, they also found that the giving of information or a contact in a benevolent, generous manner were the two most common and significant signals that someone could be trusted.

We believe that this kind of generosity can work in our favour for another important reason as well. It gives our self-esteem an instant boost, as does the gratitude that usually follows. So generosity has the power to strengthen our confidence from the inside out.

But can anyone make themselves more generous?

Many people believe that a generous spirit is 'a gift from the gods'. You are either blessed or you are not. People are born destined either to be one of life's saints or its selfish sinners. Scientists may offer genetic studies to prove their point. Others will show you a group of playing toddlers and point out that some children are demonstrably more generous than others. They share their toys willingly while others will selfishly guard their possessions and resist all attempts to coax them into giving.

We accept that that there may be a good deal of truth in these theories. But we would argue that, even if you have had the misfortune to be overloaded with selfish genes, there is no need to acquiesce to your predisposition. You can still train yourself to network like a saint rather than a sinner. So, no excuses. Persevere with these tips and you'll have everyone inviting you to sit on their lap!

Tips for building genuine generosity

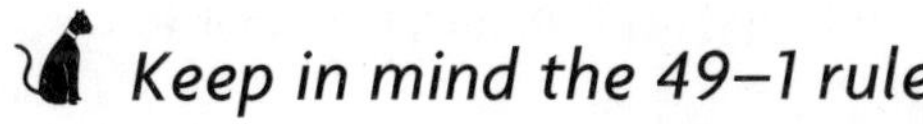

Keep in mind the 49–1 rule

This is a tip from Thomas Power, chairman of Ecademy:

> *'When you meet with someone ask them this question: "Who can I put you in touch with who can help you with your project, be that suppliers, clients or investors?"*
>
> *Repeat this process with everyone you meet and network with. Ask for nothing in return. I repeat, ask for nothing in return.*
>
> *When you meet with 50 people and have given 49 connections to those people, you will receive a contact for yourself that results in a contract for your products, services or expertise. 1,000 face to face meetings using this giving approach results in 20 contracts for your services. I continue to meet 1,000 people each year, 20 a week and have so far met 7,000 Ecademy members since 1998.'*

Ask more frequently what people need

Hopefully you have already started to do this. Remember in chapter 2, in the Self-belief Appeal exercise on pages 37–41, you were seeking information about the other person's need so that you could find a way to appear more appealing to them. In this one, you are asking questions in order to find out how you can be of assistance without any immediate benefit to you. This means that you will be listening with different ears and will select out different information to pick up on. For example:

You: 'How long have you been working in the North West?'

Contact: 'It's two years this summer – though I still feel a newcomer.'

You: 'A newcomer? Is that because you still don't know that many people here? If so, perhaps I can introduce you to a few more. I have lived in the area most of my life.'

 *Say that your gift has no strings attached*

When you give a contact, advice or a free or discounted service, make it explicit that you do not expect a favour in return. Making such a statement is more for your benefit than theirs. It will reinforce the working principle in your mind and make you feel good for acting on it. The fact that it will also ease the embarrassment factor for the other person and may make them more inclined to help you in the future would be a bonus.

 *Reward yourself for special and unappreciated acts of kindness*

When you have been especially generous, give yourself one of the rewards from the list you made earlier (pages 71–2). This is even more important if your generosity did not receive the immediate appreciation you feel it deserved. This can, and will, happen sometimes. Rewarding yourself will prevent you from wallowing in emotional hurt. It will work even better if you also remind yourself that there are many reasons why someone may not thank you enough. Firstly, some people are quite taken aback when they receive help without any apparent strings attached. If they are not used to such generosity, they may feel suspicious of your motive. Secondly, many people just feel plain embarrassed when they are not able to return a favour.

Thirdly, the person may be culturally programmed to be restrained. In the UK, where so many people are inept at handling uncomfortable feelings, you certainly may not be as effusively thanked as you would be in a more demonstrative American or Latin culture.

Finally, another reason why you may not be thanked as much as you deserve is that the other person may not be able to appreciate the value of what you have just given them. For example, they may not realise how hard and long you had to network before getting an audience with the impressive contact you have just given them.

Help others become more confident

This should be one of the easiest ways to help others after you have finished reading this book. When you see someone else struggling with some of the same issues you have experienced, you will now recognise their plight much more quickly. So not only will you be able show genuine empathy, you will also be able to give them some practical coping tips. At the moment, it may still seem like a tall order. But after a couple of months of following the tips yourself, you should feel much more confident and eager to help. (There is advice on how to help effectively in Wise Owl Know-how, chapter 16, page 248.)

 *Don't become a martyr in your efforts to be saintly*

Here is the good news! You are not required to sacrifice yourself, or your career, on the altar of networking. On the contrary, if ever your generous behaviour is becoming self-destructive, we would advise you to immediately reflect and take stock. There is a big difference between investing time, money and goodwill and wasting your life. If you feel that your efforts in a particular network are not giving you any return at all (e.g. you believe it is more like 200/0 rather than Thomas Power's 49/1 experience), change your network and find one that is more rewarding and enjoyable to be in. Networking should never drain you. If it causes you to be a burnt-out and bitter person, you are in the wrong networks!

6

Unashamed humility

YOU MAY NEVER BEFORE HAVE considered humility to be a personal quality you need to maintain or develop. You may even think you are too humble for your own good and that is why you are reading this book! So you may be surprised to hear that, in our opinion, people who lack confidence are vulnerable to illusions of superiority. Let us explain.

Humility is the direct opposite of arrogance. An illusion shared by arrogant people is that they are perfect or, at the very least, capable of reaching perfection. We believe that very many people who lack confidence are also often driven by perfectionism. We say this because we often observe them leading a self-punitive, 'No rest for the wicked' style of life. We also notice that, even when they are blatantly successful, much of their talk will continue to centre around their other failings and failures and how they 'could have done better'. Both these behaviours may appear to be signs of humility. But we suggest that their true psychological driver is perfectionism, with a slight tinge of arrogance. This becomes particularly clear when, almost inevitably, they start expecting the same high standards from others and indicate intolerance of anyone who chooses to be 'good enough' as their preferred life principle. The inference we draw from this attitude is that they consider themselves and their standards to be in some way superior. When, in the confines of a confidential coaching session, we have an opportunity to confront our clients with this often well-hidden aspect of their mind-set, they are horrified. They are horrified because at heart they are humble and respect this personal quality.

Why is humility a crucial quality of confidence?

Without humility we cannot be ourselves or fully value who we really are. We will either deny or reject parts of ourselves. For the maintenance of our inner confidence we need to be able to love ourselves in the way most parents aim to love their children – unconditionally. This does not mean that we have to like all aspects of ourselves or that we shouldn't continue to try to correct our correctable faults. It simply means that we do not reject, demean or undervalue the whole because a few of its aspects are undesirable. We do not, for example, rubbish ourselves as a networker simply because we are not very good at small talk or left some important people off our Christmas card list. Instead, as a confident person, we reflect and assess what happened, or didn't happen, in a rational objective manner. Then, as a result, we make a choice about what to do or what not to do. Such as:

- embark on training to improve our weakness

- take steps to rectify or make amends for any damage we may have done to others or to our self-esteem or to our reputation or relationships and then move on
- make positive plans to avoid situations where we know the failings we cannot or do not wish to change may let us or others down
- seek advice and help if we are unclear about what to do ourselves.

But you don't have to wait until you get it wrong before trying to get it right! You can strengthen your humility straight away by trying out these tips. Remember, truly Cool Cats know their limitations. They don't leap on to branches that won't hold their weight and they don't wander off in directions where there is no food.

Tips for strengthening your unashamed humility

Make a list of 'Impossible goals for me'

This next exercise will certainly kick-start your humility into action should it need it. But, to ensure that it doesn't go into overdrive, set a limit for your list. Your aim is to feel comfortable with it so that you are more accepting of the limits to your talents and potential. It is a real test of your unconditional love for yourself!

Kick-start your list with one or two obvious examples of challenges that are obviously impossible for you – something like climbing Everest would do. Over the next month add some more 'everyday' ones as you notice yourself wishing you could achieve something that is clearly out of your reach or putting yourself down for not being as good as someone who is out of your league in some respect or other.

You decide to buy a more up-to-date suit for an event you are going to and in the shop see someone a good deal younger than you trying one on. You think it looks great but when you try it on the buttons won't meet the button holes:	'I cannot achieve 25-year-old fitness levels now that I am 45.'
You have just been talking to an impressive contact who heads up her own highly successful consultancy. She has been eulogising about the joys of self-employment and saying how glad she is she took the risk:	'I cannot be a successful solo-entrepreneur; I function at my best as a member of a team.'
On your e-networking club site someone has just posted a dream job opportunity in a leading-edge environment. It has been a dream for you to work in this field. But a key aspect of this job requires project management skills which you do not have:	'Project implementation will never be my strength (even though I am an innovative thinker)'

 *Remind yourself of the dangers of being perceived as arrogant*

Shy and unconfident people are often seen as stand-offish. This is why you may need to make more of an effort than most people to display your humility (in a confident manner of course). This exercise will motivate you to do so.

Note down the price that you could pay should you lose some of your humility or be perceived as arrogant (even though you are not). Here are some examples:

- people could be fearful of me and not approach me
- people may not feel comfortable sharing their faults and mistakes openly with me
- I could waste time, energy and money chasing impossible dreams because people may be reluctant to face me with my mistakes or weaknesses
- people may not come forward with offers of help because they will not think I need any.

Be willing, and able, to openly share your limitations

This is the secret to being able to survive criticism as well as a way of bolstering your humility. But you must be careful that when you do share weaknesses you do so in a confident manner and not in a way that will damage your self-esteem, demean you in others' eyes or embarrass or irritate them. Here are some classic examples of ways not to share weaknesses that we have heard people who lack confidence use. (NB The tone that accompanies this kind of sharing is often whiny.)

- exaggerating (e.g. 'I'm a lost cause when it comes to making conversation')
- responding to a compliment with an unnecessary self-put down (e.g. 'Well maybe I did OK today but I made an excuse and chickened out of attending the international conference last month')

- saying you wish you were more like someone else (e.g. 'I wish I was more like you. You always seem so calm and confident')
- inviting sympathy or rescue (e.g. 'I'm too shy, don't you think?').

If you do decide to share a weakness, do so simply and directly in a matter-of-fact tone that indicates that you accept it and are actively working on it. If appropriate you could ask for help in overcoming it. You could also tag on a sentence that shares a strength or a success. Here are some examples of weaknesses shared in ways that conveyed humility without damaging confidence.

> *'I know that I am not at my best in large unstructured events so I go to courses and talks. I make great contacts that way.'*
>
> *'I was listening to a programme on the radio last week about time management and it reminded me that this is a weakness I must get to grips with. I vowed to get to more events before they start as I often miss the first speaker. So this is why I was here so early today.'*
>
> *'When I meet someone interesting, I have a tendency to get so engrossed in the conversation that I am not aware that they are trying to move on, so would you please tell me straight when you would like to do so?'*

Make a list of your weaknesses. Script out a confident way of sharing these and aim to practise slipping them into conversations over the next couple of weeks in a confident, cool manner.

Worry, but don't over-worry, about what people think of you

Here is some good news! In networking it is actually advantageous to be the kind of person who cares what others think of them. You want people to like you because you are aiming to build long-term social relationships based on mutual respect and trust. So this usually means that people who lack confidence start with an advantage in this respect because they are usually concerned about what others think of them. But, as you probably know already you can easily become overly concerned. This may cause you to stay too long with people with whom you have no hope of having a good connection; tolerating disrespectful behaviour or clamming up or putting on a 'false act' in front of potentially great friends just because you want them to like you too much or too instantly.

So you must stay in control of your urge to be liked. Here's how to do this in the early stages of a relationship.

- When you first notice yourself feeling a little too concerned about whether someone is taking to you or not, first, give yourself a positive 'talking to'. Tell yourself that this is a good sign. It shows that you care and want to connect and must ensure that you do so in a constructive and genuine way. This is an alternative to telling yourself not to worry, which is a commonly used but ineffective coping strategy.
- Switch off your physiological panic button by de-stressing your body. You can do this quickly and discreetly by slowly squeezing and uncurling your fingers or toes and deepening your breathing. If you are e-networking, you may have more time and privacy to use other relaxation techniques.

- Once you have regained your cool, actively do something (rather than just hope and worry), which will make you more genuinely likeable. This could be simply smiling, listening more attentively or indicating concern for the other's situation or needs. Alternatively, if you are ace at telling stories, recount an upbeat one or if you have some helpful information, share it. Research has shown that each of these actions increases our likeability.[2]

- Curb any urge to give free advice in order to gain favour unless it is directly requested. Even when you are asked for it, play safe by saying 'You could try X but without knowing the full details I can't be sure that would be your best plan.' It is safest (and more professional, of course) to wait until you have established a relationship of mutual respect before advising anyone.

If, after all your efforts, the other person doesn't warm to you, move on quickly. Don't hang about and wallow in your rejection. Tell yourself you can reflect later and continue networking. Once you have gained some distance from the experience, you will be better able to judge whether or not you really need that person or need to know why they don't like you.

If the person you were hoping would like you is someone with whom you are keen to make a connection, summon up the courage and ask for feedback. Try to find out why they are resisting building a relationship with you. This may sound hard, if not impossible, to do at the moment. But soon you will be learning how to reinforce your courage and then later in this book we will be introducing you to a strategy you can use to make asking for this kind of feedback much easier (Buzzy Bee Skills, chapter 12, pages 200–11).

 *Ask that 'stupid' question*

This is a tip for the occasions when you start to feel an outsider in a group conversation. Everyone else is in full flow and they appear to know something you don't. You stop yourself from asking what you have missed or don't know. You don't want to appear stupid.

But the probable reality is that you are not the only one who is struggling to keep up with the thread or understand the jargon. And even if you are the only one, you still have every right to ask.

Remind yourself that asking for clarification is a good exercise for your humility, a useful test of your confidence and that the usual responses to such requests are apologetic, helpful and inclusive.

 *Seek support overtly and expertly*

We believe almost everyone in the world suffers confidence problems from time to time. If it was more acceptable to 'go public' as soon as we felt the first butterflies and ask for support, most of us wouldn't become so held back or distressed by them. It would also be so much easier for people with more serious issues with confidence to request and receive help.

Mike, an ex-commercial director of a global blue-chip business made this point with great humility in a recent email to Stuart:

> *'There came a time (I think after my third or fourth rejection, for a role that I was technically perfect for), when I realised that I, Mike, the Font of all knowledge and superior corporate being, probably needed some help. The truly ironic thing was*

that once I embraced the idea and acted upon it, no one refused me.'

In our experience people who lack confidence often make their requests for help in the wrong way to the wrong people. The negative outcomes that result reinforce, of course, their reluctance to admit their neediness. Use the following guidelines to check that you are asking for help in a manner that will get a good response either now or in the future.

Helping others to help you

- Check availability – before you start your request, try to find out if the person has the time and energy to listen. Don't just wait until the 'right moment' when a burst of courage hits you; choose a time that will be convenient for the other person, e.g. 'I'd like 10 minutes to talk through a problem I need help with. If you think you could spare the time, would tomorrow be convenient or could you suggest ...'
- Give them an easy opt-out – make it clear that you will understand if they are unable to help and assure them that they are not your only or last resort – no one person ever is, although it may feel like that sometimes, e.g. 'Please feel free to say "No". I am sure that I could find some other source of help even though you would be my first choice.'
- Say why you have chosen them – yes, a bit of flattery does stimulate generosity. And why not? Helpers are as human as you, e.g. 'because I admire the confidence with which you circulate around a room'.

- Be boldly brief – a long history about the whys and wherefores of your problem is unnecessary and can be irritating (even to seasoned therapists!). A simple statement is often all that is needed, e.g. 'Since being made redundant, I have lost some confidence and would appreciate …'
- Focus on a specific – it would be a tall order to ask most people to help you 'become more confident'. On the other hand, a request for help with one small aspect of your problem is usually considered to be a reasonable request. Give a time frame and choose one of these areas that you need to develop and boost, e.g. 'Over the next month/few weeks I would appreciate some feedback on my body language.'
- Suggest how they could help – if you have an idea of what they could do that would be useful, spell it out. You can always ask for their ideas as well, e.g. 'I have been told that I tend to cover my mouth with my hand when I am nervous. Could you let me know when you see me doing this? But I'd also be grateful for any other feedback that you think might help me as well.'

Stay an eternal student

Keep learning new information and skills high on your priority list. Most of us lead very busy lives today, and it is tempting to cut down on studying when we need a particular qualification. Keeping yourself in some kind of a learning role will keep you humble and the bonus is that your confidence will be further boosted when you achieve results. Our Wise Owl Know-how section will give you many ideas and leads.

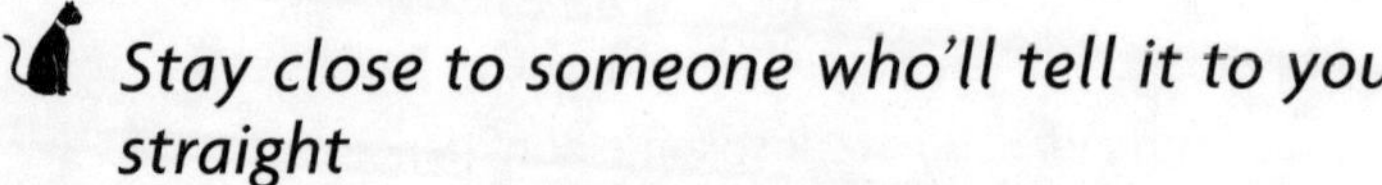

Stay close to someone who'll tell it to you straight

Make sure you have someone close to you in your life who is assertive enough to cut you back down to size should you show signs of arrogance.

Being married to each other has certainly been our best protection for years!

7

Calculated courage

LET'S START BY SCARING YOU! Here are some fearsome facts:

1. All people are unpredictable
2. People you don't know are even less predictable than those you do know
3. Networking is an activity involving both people you know and don't know.

These facts may not be news to you, but do you avoid facing them? Do you stick as close as you can to 'the devils' you think you know? Isn't it true that, given a choice, you would almost always choose to spend an evening with old acquaintances, rather than go to an event where you will be faced with a sea of unknown faces? Isn't it also true that you would still be inclined to make this choice even if the old faces were predictably boring, or had changed into people you no longer need or want to be with?

In making such choices, you are conning yourself into a false sense of security. Every single human relationship is risky; each and every one has a certain amount of potential to surprise us both pleasantly and unpleasantly. Successful networkers are just as vulnerable as you are. They hurt as much as any other human when they are rejected, disappointed and let down by people. Their financial health and career prospects are put just as much on the line as yours when networking. Often a simple difference between them and less confident novices is that they have more courage. That is why they can take more risks. And, of course, they choose to take risks, because in networking the more you take, the more rewards you can reap.

No one; but no one, is magically endowed with a steel heart. Courage is a personal quality that has to be built. Through networking we recently had the privilege of meeting a highly inspirational model of courage, Giles Long (www.gileslong.com).

Giles is a 28-year-old British Paralympic swimmer with seven medals to his name, including three gold ones. At 13 he was well on the road to a highly successful career in swimming in the non-disabled field. One day when playing a knock-around game of football, he fell and broke his arm. This accident revealed serious bone cancer. A good proportion of his next few years was spent having painful operations and other treatments. He told us that on many occasions his courage would disappear almost completely. But with the help of a particularly encouraging and wise coach, he learned how to boost and maintain it to such a degree that not only did it support him to excel in the Paralympics but he can now depend on its support when he faces audiences of hundreds in his new role as a motivational speaker. He believes, as we do, that there is a strong link between courage and confidence:

> *'Knowing now that I can pull courage out of the bag any time when I may need it feeds my confidence – and having confidence means that I have even more courage when I need it.'*

So courage has to be built, but then, in order for it to be dependable, it has to be constantly exercised and maintained. If it is not, it will erode away. People who have been unexpectedly made redundant from what they thought was a safe job soon face this truth. Most we meet are taken by surprise at how suddenly fearful they find themselves. They often recall times in their past when they have had immense courage and hate themselves for now feeling so anxious about networking. These quotes from two of our clients illustrate this phenomenon:

> *'I remember when I left college and set about job hunting, I was fearless. I can remember walking straight into the reception of a company I was keen to work for, and asking to speak to the person in charge of recruitment. That's how I got my first job. Now I'd be very nervous about making such a direct approach.*
>
> Jim, *project manager in the construction industry*

> *'I can't believe that in the job I had before I had the children, I regularly gave presentations to groups of 200 or more and here I am shaking as I am trying to tell this small group about my previous career achievements.'*
>
> Marie, *a pharmaceutical research scientist*

One of the world's heroes Nelson Mandela would undoubtedly empathise. It must have been a personal hell for him to have to face the world after so many years of comparative isolation on Robben Island. Most people admire him for the immense courage he has shown in the face of physical risk, but we admire him even more for the risks he has had to take in relation to being with people. He is, by nature, a shy person who has had to (and still has to in his eighties!) force himself to take a leading place on the world stage. His autobiography was inspirational for Gael after the death of our 19-year-old daughter. Having hidden away from the world for months in her grief, she felt fearful of going back into her public life leading groups and giving talks and media interviews. Reading these words written by Mandela in our Spanish hideaway was a turning point: 'I felt fear myself more times than I can remember, but I hid it under a mask of boldness. The brave man is not he who does not feel afraid, but he who conquers that fear.'

How do we conquer fear? By taking risks, of course! But not in a brash way. Plunging yourself blindly into the deep end of terror is not recommended. Cool Cats take a much more calculated approach. Our tips are designed to gradually build up your courage rather than push you all paws forward into the lion's den.

Tips for building calculated courage

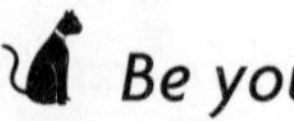 *Be your own judge and jury*

No one else may ever understand your fears. No one else can ever appreciate just how risky a risk is for you. You have probably had a lifetime's advice from people who have told you that you 'shouldn't' be afraid of what is frightening you. Maybe they are right, maybe there is no good rational reason for quaking in your shoes before you pick up the telephone to ring certain types of people or walk through the door of certain kinds of offices. But, maybe they are wrong. You could be the one who is right. You are probably right to be afraid of those kinds of situations because you are in danger – in danger of behaving like a helpless victim! The risk factor for you could therefore be ten times higher than for someone else.

When building courage, therefore, we must only listen and respect our own inner signals of fear. The next time someone tells you that you shouldn't be frightened of doing something, simply say: 'Perhaps I shouldn't, but I am' or 'Maybe you wouldn't be frightened, but I am.' If they persist, just add: 'I prefer to deal with my fear rather than deny it exists.' They'll soon leave you in peace. You're better off without that kind of advice, however well meaning it may be. But don't forget you can still ask for their support. The vast majority of people will want to help you build your courage although they may not know the best way to do so, nor even that you are in need of their help.

Don't worry too much about your fear being on show

Scott Allen, co-author of *The Five Keys to Building Business Relationships On-line*, says in his experience in networking, displaying uncertainty can sometimes even help because it makes people want to help you more. Most people are kind and won't hold your show of nerves against you. This is especially true if they see you persisting through your fear with courage. It is our experience too that voicing fear often brings unexpected empathy. Try it. The next time you are feeling nervous, for example at the start of a function, you could say to a neighbour, 'I find these kinds of meetings somewhat daunting.' We doubt that you'll receive a response of either surprise or horror. You are more likely to hear sympathetic acknowledgement, and may even be given some constructive help.

Being overly keen not to look or sound nervous will just make you even more self-conscious and unable to concentrate on the subject of the conversation.

Similarly in e-networking, if you are nervous about making contact with someone and you write as though you are already superbly confident, you may get a brusque brush-off response designed for someone with a thicker skin than you. If, however, you own up assertively to your diffidence (e.g. 'I have been trying to pluck up the courage to write to you for the last few months and now I have finally made it! I wanted to know if you would ...') you may get a much more encouraging and more carefully thought-through response.

 *Stop avoiding 'safe' risks*

The risks we are referring to are risks in relation to meeting and interacting with people when you are networking. For example, you may avoid making approaches to potentially good contacts or be too guarded in your conversation because you are afraid of:

- being ignored
- being let down
- being forgotten
- being rejected

- being boring
- being judged as silly or stupid
- becoming overemotional
- letting someone else or your company down
- getting someone's name wrong (or other important data)
- 'drying up' due to anxiety
- wasting someone's time.

If any of these examples ring bells for you, you are limiting your opportunities. You are probably also damaging your self-esteem by telling yourself what a coward you are because you see other people taking these risks all the time. Remember that if this behaviour has become a habit, it is probably one you developed originally to protect yourself when you were emotionally vulnerable for one reason or other. Its start could date as far back as childhood or it could have started more recently after a hurt from a serious setback or relationship breakdown. Kicking yourself for being 'childish' or 'stupid' won't help but replacing this self-sabotaging avoidance habit with the next two tips will.

Do a more daring dare each week

For the next two months set yourself a dare for each week. Start with one that is relatively easy and gradually increase the risk factor until by the end of the two-month period you have achieved something worthy of a celebration. Remember when goal-setting that both those that are too daunting for your current level of courage and goals that are far too easy are as bad as each other.

- Make a list of situations, people or events that hold some degree of fear for you. Then grade each, using, for example a 1–10 scale.
- Select eight of these ranging from the mildly anxiety provoking, such as sending a fan email to someone you admire but consider 'above your station', to the most difficult, such as trying to sell yourself to a senior someone you need to impress.
- Set yourself a specific dated goal for each month. Each one should be slightly more challenging than the last.
- After the first month, reassess. You may need to change a goal or two according to the progress you are making.

Tame your inner taunts with snappy self-talk

As soon as the inner negative devil within you gets up to its tricks, drown out its voice immediately. Repeat, preferably out loud, a few self-affirming statements in a calm Cool Cat voice such as: 'I am courageous'; 'I can handle my anxiety'; 'I will not let fear stop me from doing what I want to do.' Experiment with different statements until you find the ones that work best for you. Then stick to using these so your brain will recognise them and instantly switch off the panic response.

An alternative to using these kinds of affirmations is to use one or two of your favourite quotes from courageous people in the same way. Here are some examples from various walks of life:

> *'Being a coward is corrosive to your self-esteem. You say to yourself, "I am going to feel better about myself than if I agreed when I shouldn't have agreed".'*
>
> Michael Feiner, *professor, Columbia Business School*

> *'You can't be brave if you have only had wonderful things happen to you.'*
>
> Mary Tyler Moore, *activist, actress and survivor of personal tragedy and disability*

> *'It is courage based on confidence, not daring, and it is confidence based on experience.'*
>
> Dr Jonas Salk *on his decision to try out his polio vaccine on himself and his family*

Take a friend rather than stay behind

In the early days of building up your courage, it is fine to lean on others for some support. Taking a friend with you to an event is better than avoiding it altogether. The support will get you through that dreaded door. Once you are in, separate. Arrange to talk after the event. Knowing that you have to report back on your progress will inspire you to be more courageous. Even if you were only able to take one small risk such as approaching a friendly looking stranger standing on their own, you will benefit from being duly congratulated.

Research the background of daunting people

There are three good reasons for finding out more about the stories behind the success of high achievers. So search the internet or library for interviews and biographical profiles of people whom you admire and with whom you would like to have contact.

Firstly, doing this will demystify them because these stories usually reveal their humanness, including their early struggles and mistakes. Secondly, it will provide you with interesting pieces of information, which you can use as conversation starters such as: 'I hope you don't mind me approaching you but I read in your profile that you have been working as a … for … years. I am thinking about training in that field and wonder if you would mind telling me where …' Thirdly, they will be extra nice to you because they will be so impressed by your knowledge about them!

 *Prepare a white-lie escape*

Although we must assess all risks as best as we can, ultimately we have to remember that networking can never, ever be risk-free. There will always be a 'plunge point'. If you give yourself prior permission to escape before you plunge, you will be more likely to do the dive. Until your confidence is more fully developed, have a small white lie at the ready to pull you out of the situation should you need it. The chances are your lie will never be heard. The vast majority of fears about networking are unfounded and irrational. This is especially true for Cool Cats who have also perfected the confidence skills of a Buzzy Bee. So let's now move courageously forward to our next section and meet even more challenges!

PART TWO

•

Buzzy Bee Skills

In this section you will learn how to develop your outer confidence. You will be developing the six key skills, which we have identified as the core social skills of Confident Networkers. Like Buzzy Bees, they are great communicators and get a buzz from enriching the world through cross-pollination. They live and work co-operatively but have hidden stings in their tails for self-protection.

8

Impact instantly with a lasting impression

IN NETWORKING, FIRST IMPRESSIONS ARE crucial. We often need to make a lasting positive impact within moments of encountering people. If we don't, we will almost certainly lose out on making valuable new connections. Opportunities can come and go in an instant. 'Speed networking' has recently become more and more commonplace even in ordinary business social events. This is when the organisers strictly limit the amount of time people spend with each other. Invariably this is only two to five minutes. Even if you choose not to do this kind of fast-paced networking yourself, others may do it even at events not specifically run for this purpose. So the person you need to make contact with may well be one of those you can now regularly see buzzing around the pub or conference refreshment area trying to meet as many people as possible in the shortest amount of time.

Then, of course, there are the chance encounters. At these you may have even less than a minute to make a positive impact. So every networker has to be ready to have snap judgements made about them based on their external image rather than their impressive CV or their beautiful inner soul.

You may remember that in chapter 2 we recounted the story of Fiona whose self-belief let her down in this respect. Here is another story of someone who, in contrast, was more than adequately endowed with inner confidence. She missed a second bite at an important networking cherry simply because her outer appearance on just one day let her down.

CASE STUDY

Jean, a highly qualified and well-respected senior manager with a marketing consultancy, had a lunch date with Deidre, an old friend and colleague. Jean arrived late in a breathless and dishevelled state. She rushed straight into the restaurant without doing her usual freshen-up and appearance check in the Ladies. She found Deidre talking to a woman she didn't know. She was introduced and learned that this person was Margaret, the marketing director of a German-based multinational. She was in London for an international sales conference they were all attending the next day. She had been on her way out of the restaurant when she spotted Deidre, a former colleague.

For some time Jean had wanted to meet a key contact from Germany. Her boyfriend had just been transferred to Stuttgart and she was about to start looking for opportunities for herself. She was planning to join him later in the year. So, the next night, knowing that she would see Margaret the next day, she pressed her best designer suit, checked she had a supply of new business cards and printed out a clean copy of her CV, which had details of her impressive track record including testimonials from several German clients. She then sent Margaret an email saying that she was pleased to have met her the previous night, and would like a few quick words with her at lunchtime the next day about opportunities in her department. (Deidre had sung Margaret's praises and said she was sure she would make time for her tomorrow.)

When Margaret saw the message from Jean flash up on her Blackberry, she immediately recalled her image of her. This was 'Tall woman with untidy hair; chipped nail polish and squeaky voice'. She sighed and thought to herself 'No, not tomorrow. I don't want to waste my own precious opportunities to network at lunch. There is no way that someone like that would fit into our team anyway. We need confident people who can function self-sufficiently.' So, she emailed Jean back to say that she was already booked up for lunch and advised her to send her CV to Human Resources.

Jean did, but (surprise, surprise!), her enquiry met with the polite standard rejection letter saying they would contact her if an opportunity arose in the future. It wasn't till a year or so later that Jean heard Margaret's side of the story via another mutual contact during her sixth visit to Stuttgart for an interview.

We may wish we didn't have to operate in a world where this kind of crude people selection takes place, but the reality is that most of us do.

First impressions are notoriously difficult to shift and can colour the way people see you forever afterwards. They act like a filter through which people view all your subsequent actions and interactions. Now that we know more about how the brain works we can understand how this happens. It's those memory-matching tricks at work once again. In its constant effort to maintain equilibrium within our system (known as the homeostasis principle) our brain scans new information. It searches to find something similar to the memory that was stored at the first impression. As a result, our senses highlight the similarities and we may not even notice the differences. This is why if you want to try and correct a bad first impression, you may have to 'shout' about your self-reinvention. If you don't, it will not make much impact on the people you have met before. (This is the 'I spent a fortune at the hairdressers last week and he still hasn't noticed!' syndrome!)

Are you going to bite the image bullet or not?

Imagine this scene and make your choice. You walk into a networking event and see two fairly distinct groups of people. Which one would you truly like to join? (And no, there is no fence to sit on!)

The Central Stagers
are confident people who are experts at making themselves memorable. They know the tricks of fast image impact and are not afraid to use them. They are happy standing in the heart of the buzzing crowd and doing what they can to be noticed. They exude charisma and individuality and enjoy receiving attention.

The Wallflowers
are unconfident people who are experts at making themselves forgettable. They may know that they could learn the tricks of image impact but have been fearful of doing so. They prefer to watch from the wings and are relieved that the others are too busy to notice their existence. They are dreading the moment they may be pulled or pushed into the centre of the action.

Let's now assume you have joined us in the centre of the networking stage – welcome!

Your next decision is to choose your image. To make a quick, strong, lasting impact, it has to be the kind that can be conveyed simply and consistently. Remember, first impressions are largely formed by the primitive subconscious. This is a part of the brain that isn't wired up for processing complicated information. It gathers its data subliminally and spontaneously through our senses, mainly from body language and general appearance factors. It then rapidly and crudely matches this with data collected from our past experiences and our established belief systems. The next exercise will illustrate this process in action.

Exercise

Use your imagination to picture yourself once again at a networking event.

A man walks briskly into a room and gives a brief firm handshake to all the people in the group with whom you are conversing. As he is doing this, your subconscious brain is taking in his:

> loud voice; reddish hair; stooped shoulders; paunch; jokey animal tie; expensive, well-tailored suit, well-worn leather briefcase

Make a snap judgement NOW. Don't think. We want a one-second decision. Ask yourself:

> 'Is this someone I would want, or need, to talk to more?'

Now examine your instant first impression of this man with your conscious brain. Ask yourself what matches it might have been making with your stored memories. To help clarify, here are some examples others have reported. Note your own beside them without thinking for more than a second or two.

First impressions:		My impressions
Loud voice	=	overbearing parent; teacher; boss
Reddish hair	=	fiery personality of school best friend
Stooped shoulders	=	stressed; too many responsibilities
Paunch	=	unfit; likes the good life
Jokey animal tie	=	eccentric; family man; sense of humour
Expensive, well-tailored suit	=	success; city professional
Well-worn leather briefcase	=	posh background; unworldly
Brief, firm handshake	=	busyness; confident

Reflect on the associations your subconscious made with this first impression. Did you or did you not make a good decision?

Your answer is probably: 'I am not sure.' A good answer perhaps, but not the point! You made a decision. And, as a result you would have either pursued a possible connection with this man or not.

So when thinking about your image, remember the networking world is full of people like you making snap judgements! You can choose to make the best or worst of this fact. It is only a matter of knowing how.

If you have the money and time, you could take yourself to an image consultant and ask for some professional advice on how best to do this. But first, try our tips.

Tips for presenting yourself with impact

Make a personal impact checklist

We suggest that you choose just three positive qualities to concentrate on projecting externally. Once you have decided which these are, memorise them! They will act as your personal checklist. You can use them for rapid reference whenever you are getting yourself ready to go out and about or, indeed, make a connection by any other means. They will help you make decisions about such matters as the clothes you wear, the business stationery you use, the body language you adopt and the words you use to introduce yourself. Here are some examples to get you started:

confident	confident	confident
credible	professional	competent
charming	approachable	connected

You will have noticed that we have included confidence as a quality in all our examples. This is because it carries universal appeal and as you have progressed this far with us, we assumed that this might be a quality you are keen to convey!

Dress up not down

The only possible exceptions to this rule may be people who are looking for downshifting opportunities. We believe most people in networking are on the opposite track so we suggest that when you network, you dress for the job you want next rather than the job you have now. But try to ensure that the clothes and accessories you choose also:

- highlight your strong and attractive features or reflect your character (e.g. blue for blue eyes and red for forcefulness)
- are appropriate for the event you are attending (you can 'dress up' a little even if it's casual wear)
- are not so brand new that they make you feel self-conscious
- aren't *so* stunning that they detract from the you inside
- have a story to tell that could give away some 'free' information about you that will help you to be remembered, as well as providing a conversation starter (e.g. 'Thank you. It is a favourite tie of mine – I bought it when I was working in Greece last year. Have you been there?').

Ask others if your actions speak as loud as your words

We all know how important body language is nowadays. In recent years we have been bombarded with articles, books and even TV programmes on the subject. So you must also know how vital it is to get it right during a first meeting. It must convey self-confidence and ensure that you are noticed and perceived in the way you deserve to be.

If your confidence has been low for some time, you will almost certainly have acquired some bad habits, such as stooping, fidgeting, scratching or covering your mouth with your hand. It is almost impossible to correct these on your own because you are rarely conscious of them. This is probably because you are too worried about what you are going to say, even though the experts reckon that words are usually only responsible for 7 per cent of a first impression!

So, you need to find others to observe you who will give you honest feedback. There may be someone else in your network with the same problem. Could you agree to observe each other? Alternatively, ask an assertive colleague for some straight-talking feedback. Once you know what these habits are you can practise using more confident body language on your own. Use a mirror to give you feedback. Focus your attention on these three factors.

Posture

- pull yourself upright by imagining a string running through from the soles of your feet to the top of your head
- put your shoulders back and down
- tighten your abdominals.

Composure

- place two feet on the ground (not crossed or hopping!)
- stop any fidgeting, fiddling, scratching or tapping
- breathe deeply and slowly – expanding your chest out rather than down to stop your shoulders lifting.

Approachability

- stand or sit at an angle – when in conversation this will signal to others that they can join in
- smile – it is a draw and is contagious!
- relax your arms – don't place them on your hips because that is a sign of dominance

- put palms up – if you start using hand gestures
- mind the gap – the generally accepted norm in networking is to maintain a 60cm distance, but this can vary from culture to culture.

Finally, don't forget that you need to practise a new habit at least 16 times before it is registered in your brain! So persist and give yourself a refresher rehearsal before you go to that important event.

Make your name memorable

If your name can be spelt more than one way, you could sometimes spell it out. Or, if you have a tale to tell around your name, you can use this to fix it in the mind of a new contact. You can then ask if there is a story about their name, and this gives you a better chance of remembering theirs as well. This kind of personal sharing is a good way to establish a bond quickly with someone. But don't overdo it, and try to ring the changes with the story! Here are a couple of our own examples:

> *'It's spelt the Irish way – G-A-E-L. It is highly individual in England but I'm much more ordinary in Ireland!'*
>
> *'Stuart is difficult for Spaniards to pronounce, so I have to answer to two names: Stuart and Estuardo.'*

Prepare a positive personal pitch

> *'What do you do?'*
>
> *'What brings you here?'*
>
> *'What line of business are you in?'*

These must be the most frequently asked questions in networking circles. At face value they may sound like easy ones to answer. But do you answer them in a way that creates an impact that will leave a lasting positive impression?

We often hear these questions answered in a flat, unimaginative way. A common mistake is to put yourself into a professional pigeon-hole along with thousands of others by just saying, for example: I am an accountant; I work for IBM; I'm a project manager in the pharmaceutical industry. Super-confident networkers rarely do this. They use well-rehearsed lines – known as 'elevator pitches' – that have been composed with the greatest of care. This is because so many opportunities to make an impression are as short-lived as those we may meet when travelling in a lift with an interesting looking stranger. A client of ours sent us this story, which illustrates this 'truth' well.

CASE STUDY

Philip, a friend of mine, last year happened to get into a lift with the CEO of a major pharmaceutical company. The CEO asked what brought him to the HQ. He explained his role and what he was doing. The CEO was so impressed he asked to meet him later. As a result of this subsequent meeting, Philip is now running a group managing a substantial part of that business. At the time he met this CEO, the area he had been working in was seriously under threat.

There were four or five layers of management between the two people, so it was unlikely that these two men would have had a one-to-one opportunity to talk in the course of their everyday working lives. You could give luck a bit of the credit for this outcome and also some to the CEO. (Successful leaders rarely miss an opportunity to scout for talent.) However, the vast majority of the credit must belong to Philip. He obviously knew how to answer that crucial question posed in the lift in a way that made an outstanding impression. He had the skill to create a life-changing opportunity for himself in a few seconds. We don't know how Philip acquired his skill, but we do know that it is one that rarely comes easily for most people. So be prepared to work at it over and over again until it feels natural to you as well as having a positive 'wow' impact on others.

We suggest that instead of preparing just one 'elevator pitch' to describe you and your work, prepare several. (Sorry, even harder work!) Varying the pitches you use will prevent your response from sounding too slick and off-pat. It also gives you an opportunity to build in some appropriate appeal factors. Practise tailoring different ones for specific environments and for different types of people. (We have listed some of our 'elevator pitches' on pages 118–20. Note that we have included our aims.) Think about your objectives before composing your lines. These could include getting across all, or just one or two of the following:

- your core strengths
- your special expertise
- your non-negotiable values
- your credibility
- your particular passion
- your energy
- your openness to new opportunities
- plus of course, your confident and positive personality!

Use a pencil or computer to write them out because you'll need to edit and re-edit them. Take care to choose words you think will appeal to your particular listener, and which convey the appropriate balance of professionalism and human emotion. As a general rule, remember the simpler it sounds, and shorter it is, the more easy on the ear it will be and the more impact it will have.

Aim for your lines to sound colloquial rather than contrived. Do not aim to be witty or overly 'punchy' with your words. The killer 'sound-bite' kind of pitches that are commonly recommended in networking books are very difficult to deliver without sounding trite and 'salesy'. Leave these to the super-confident extroverts who can cope with the even wittier response or the 'glazed look' they may provoke!

Also, do not replace your professional 'label' with anything too obviously sales-orientated. For example, instead of financial adviser, don't say 'I am a wealth creator.' Instead, even if it takes a few extra words, replace this with a brief description of what you do and what your specialism is and how it helps others, for example, instead of financial adviser, say 'I advise people, especially those working for themselves, on how to save and invest' – that's much clearer.

When you have composed your pitches, test them out with several people. Start with people you know and trust, but also try to get feedback from people who are not familiar with your line of work. Don't forget to spell out your aims before saying each of your pitches, and accompany the words with confident and energetic body language.

It is generally advisable to learn your pitches off by heart so they trip off the tongue easily and you can concentrate on the even more important aspect of a first impression, body language. But as you grow in confidence, you can allow yourself room to improvise. Keep your key impact phrases, but change the words that you use to link these together. Skilled theatre actors use this trick all the time to prevent their performances becoming stilted.

Gael's 'elevator pitches':

1. For a business social event: 'For the past 20 years my day job has been writing self-help books – specialising in confidence and managing feelings. When I am not chaining myself to my computer, I also give talks, lead courses, talk to the media and, thankfully, I also still do some individual consultations.'

   My aim was to:

   - establish credibility as an author (20 years suggests a successful track record)
   - convey humanness (need to be chained to computer)
   - give impression of being in demand and still full of energy (even at my time of life!)
   - indicate that I still care about and stay in touch with real-life problems of individuals.

2. For a professional conference: 'I write personal development books and lead seminars on subjects such as *Super Confidence*, *Managing Anger* and *Success from Setbacks*. My most recent publication is *Confident Networking* – a very challenging project as it is the first joint one with my husband, Stuart.'

   My aim was to:

   - sound professional and authoritative (give punchy titles of books they may recognise)

- indicate my key specialities and suggest relevant skill (i.e. seminars)
- convey warmth and humanness (I would smile as I say 'challenging')
- give a hook for an engaging response ('Do you also run seminars on Confident Networking?' or 'How brave! I couldn't see me doing something like that with my wife/husband. It would drive us to the divorce courts').

Stuart's 'elevator pitches':

1. For a business social event: 'I run the South-East operation for a world-leading career management company where I specialise in helping people take better control of their careers. I have a lot of experience of delivering popular networking workshops and talks. I get a real buzz from seeing the transformational impact these workshops can have.'

   My aim was to:

   - appear credible (running operation – world-leading company)
   - clarify my specialism
   - show that I am a 'buzzy' person!
   - refer to the positive impact of my workshops – likely to prompt a response like 'What kind of people attend these?' or 'What types of 'transformations' occur?'

2. For a less formal social event: 'Through 1-1s and networking workshops, I help people take better control of their careers. I've run lots of popular workshops and given many keynote speeches on networking, and now I'm co-authoring

a book *Confident Networking* with my wife – my first – her 19th!'

My aim was to:

- describe my areas of expertise
- show that I'm busy and in demand (lots of workshops, many keynote speeches)
- add credibility through new book and prompt a response (such as checking out what it's like to produce a book jointly with your spouse!)

Finally, before going anywhere important, take a tip from the great actor Laurence Olivier. Practise in front of the mirror. He is reputed to have said that he knew he had got a speech right when he could look at himself doing it without falling about laughing.

Summon up energy to convey passion

We were recently told by the director of an agency specialising in first impressions in the business arena that energy is the magic ingredient that makes the most powerful impact. Without energy you cannot convey passion and it is above all your passion that will 'sell' you and make you memorable.

Many networking events are held after a busy day at work. So you may not be feeling very energetic. So before going to an event, take time out to rest and do some quick relaxation exercises to re-charge you. If you can find the time and private space, close your eyes for 30 seconds and visualise yourself talking passionately and energetically about your work. This will kick-start the production of the extra adrenalin you need.

Take charge of your badge

There are some common problems we have encountered with badges we have been given at events, from names being spelt wrongly or illegibly, to descriptions of you being inappropriate or incomplete. Badges will typically simply state your position, and not how you might benefit the audience, limiting your chances of 'instant appeal' and automatic conversation openers when you meet others.

A solution to some of these problems can be to ring the organisers beforehand and check the information is correct. But they may be hard to contact and have a standard format that they are reluctant to change for one badge. We suggest you always keep a spare badge of your own in your briefcase or pocket. You will stand out for being different and you can make sure that it is as you wish it to be. Your badge could, for example, include an appealing 'strapline' – a catchy line that captures the essence of your role or business, or reflects your key value or mission. But, before wearing it, it is good manners, of course, to check with the organisers that they do not mind you wearing your own. We have rarely encountered a 'no'.

Carry cards that are personal and provoking

Whenever possible, ensure that your business cards are in tune with your personal image. Many of you will have been allocated business cards by your company. Even if you cannot change the overall design, you may be able to persuade them to allow you to include a personal strapline. Stuart's managed to get his company to agree to including his strapline on his card ('Helping You Take Control of Your Career').

Many people now carry several different cards. Some are in

different languages for international networking. Some are separate cards for personal use. If you think your company business card is not in tune with your real image, this could be an option. Nowadays cards can be designed and produced very cheaply so it would be well worth a small investment, especially if you are considering a career or job move, or are involved in impressive or interesting projects in your personal time.

Another option is to go much more upmarket with your card. You can choose cards that are glossy and high quality; eco-friendly handmade paper; over-sized; laminated; produced on a credit-card size CD and clear plastic. It is also now becoming increasingly common to use both sides of the card, which is a cost-effective way to give more impact and information. Gael has examples of the books she has written and courses she runs on the back of hers.

The design of your card will depend on the nature of your business. It might be creative in its design if you are selling innovative products or services and more traditional if you are in a profession such as accounting, law or medicine. The same is true of any personal logo that you might choose. But don't forget that the general rules for memorable impact still apply – keep it simple as well as striking and personalised.

Don't forget to check out the etiquette before handing out business cards. This varies from country to country. In some you should never ask for a card from a senior person until they have offered theirs to you; in others you must never put them in your back pocket or write on them. In Japan, you must hand and receive cards with two hands and bow as you do and then spend time reading the card. In the UK things are much more informal and the exchange involves little ceremony. When in doubt, play safe – at the very least hold the card for a moment while looking at it. If you read some information out loud from it and comment on it, it will indicate interest and respect and also will help fix the person more firmly in your mind. You could say 'Oh it says Oxford – a wonderful place.' Or 'Innovative consulting – that sounds interesting.'

Take a talking point

At some events you can try carrying or wearing something that will provoke conversation. Here are some examples of ones that we know have worked:

- a foreign newspaper
- daily newspaper with latest dramatic sports headline
- a company or trade or hobby journal
- a book (but you should have read it first!)
- a striking handbag
- bits and pieces in a bag with a foreign airline or airport logo
- a buttonhole such as a daffodil for St David's Day or shamrock on St Patrick's Day
- a bottle of champagne in a container with carrying handle (excuse to say what you have done that deserves a celebration).

But don't forget to prepare a memorable story or nugget of information to go with whatever you choose.

Keep your confidence well boosted

Remember all the work you are doing in this book will help with your impact. Confidence in itself grabs attention and attracts people to you.

> *'People who exude confidence, but not overpoweringly so, are like a magnet in the room.'*
>
> Scott Allen, *co-author of Make Your Business Click: How to Value and Grow Your Network*

9

Conversing with confidence

CONVERSATIONS! HAVE WE AT LAST reached the heart of the problem?

We wouldn't be surprised to learn that this is how it feels for you. Having to make conversation with people you don't know in unfamiliar situations with no specific agenda and no designated 'leader' could even be your idea of hell! Perhaps your heart is palpitating at the very thought of it right now. We hope to lessen your fear considerably, but we can't promise to transform it into exhilarating excitement. This aspect of networking may never hold great appeal for you. This is especially true if you are an introvert by nature. However, after learning and practising a few simple techniques, you will find networking conversations much easier and more productive.

Conversation is often referred to as an 'art'. But in reality it is a set of skills and that is how you should think of it. It is not a 'God-given' gift. People are not 'blessed' with it when they are born, as they might be with an extraordinarily beautiful voice or a talent for drawing. It is a set of behaviours, like driving a car, riding a bike or managing a computer.

Conversation shares with all skills these attributes:

- the earlier in your life you learn them, the more 'natural' and effortless the behaviour feels and the easier they are to pick up again if they have gone 'rusty'
- the more you understand how they work and are aware of the step-by-step process by which they are learned, the easier they are to acquire
- the more you practise and repeat them, the more competent you will become at using them
- some people enjoy learning particular skills (e.g. perfectionists like learning law and extroverts like learning to converse) but all skills can be learned to some degree by anyone (unless a severe physical disability makes this impossible)
- the more you want to learn and the more rewarding you make the process of learning, the quicker the skills are acquired.

So, no more excuses! You can learn to be a good-enough conversationalist; it is only a matter of understanding a bit more about how it works and practising. Once the skill is learned, as Mike, a human resources director we know said, it will serve as a kind of social insurance for life.

> *Most of the things I believe in, and most of the good ideas I have had, have been picked up, magpie like, through conversation. But good conversation can also have a dramatic impact on your success in business. I remember, with affection, a training manager on my team who was*

willing and able to converse with anyone. He had that rare blend of self-confidence and a genuine interest in people that endeared him to others.

He subsequently became the casualty of a reorganisation, and despite a lifelong career in the corporate world, decided to start his own business. How did he do? Instant success! Within a month of starting, his business was fully established, with an order book that was the envy of his competitors. Why? – Because of his extensive network of relationships, built upon conversations.

Mike Batcheler, *Director of HR, Novartis Pharmaceuticals UK*

First it may help to take an analytical look at social conversation. As you will see in our guide below, on pages 128–32, there are five different levels of conversation to consider. A good conversationalist has simply learned how and when to glide between these levels.

When starting new relationships, it is usually advisable to move consciously and tentatively through each different level, stopping at the one you judge to be most appropriate for the relationship and which appears to be comfortable for both parties. In business networking you may never move from Level 1 with the majority of people you meet. Until it feels natural, you can use this summarised guide for carrying out occasional spot-checks to ensure that you are operating at the right conversational level with the new connections you have in your network. Remember, when in doubt, you can always backtrack. It is better than moving forward too fast – that can seriously damage a relationship. But keep cool – it is not that difficult! Making conversation is in essence a rudimentary skill – in spite of our attempts to give it some theory! It is not an exact science any more than it is a mystical art. And furthermore our extra extensive tips in this section will equip you with all the practical knowledge you need to be able to glide effortlessly from level to level.

The five levels of social conversation in business networking

Level 1: Small talking

General conversation about subjects such as the weather, sport, holidays, journeys, venues, food or uncontroversial news stories. Its usual form is to make an innocuous statement and then follow it with an inoffensive question on a safe subject.

Uses:

- first meetings
- observing body language and assessing general image
- 'oiling the wheels' of relationships between newly established connections
- exploring the possibilities of developing the relationship on to a more personal footing by safely sounding out the other person's personality style, general cultural background and areas of interest
- lightening the mood or emotional tone after an overly 'heavy' conversation
- keeping relationships on a strictly professional footing when there is a danger of them becoming too personal or keeping inappropriate sexual feelings at bay.

Examples:

> *'It's hot today – I thought it was supposed to rain.'*
>
> *'This train seems to get more crowded each day. But it looks at least as though we'll make it on time.'*
>
> *'This hotel is looking a bit jaded – I wonder if it is due for a make-over – or indeed a take-over. Which is your favourite venue in . . .?'*

Level 2: Selective self-disclosing

Revealing 'safe' personal information (not your deepest feelings or intimate details) about yourself, your experiences and interests. This is usually gently dropped into small talk.

This level can be used as:

- a tentative experiment with a possible new contact
- a signal of your willingness to move the conversation on to a more 'friendly' level
- a way of maintaining a relaxed and trusting relationship with a less confident or socially skilled person until they are ready to reveal themselves more.

Examples:

> *'When I moved to Birmingham, eight years ago. . .'*
>
> *'The last time I came here was when I was setting up my business four years ago. . .'*
>
> *'When I heard the news this morning, I was shocked to hear that. . .'*

Level 3: Polite probing

Active listening and questioning the other person for 'safe' information about themselves, after they have shown an interest in your self-disclosure or self-disclosed themselves.

Uses:

- finding areas of mutual interest
- eliciting useful practical and factual information
- prompting sharing from a shy person whom you guess wants to develop the friendship but only at a 'safe' pace.

Examples:

'Do you know many people here?'

'I've just returned from a working week in Saigon. Does your business involve travelling?

'You know when I was first introduced to you I had a sense that I had seen you before. Were you by any chance at…'

Level 4: Testing for trust

Giving compliments; asking questions and making statements that reveal personal feelings and values or information on personal life and asking for introductions and sounding out general ideas.

Uses:

- finding out whether there is enough compatibility to build a friendship

- finding out whether there is enough trust and mutual respect to start a business relationship
- declaring your esteem or liking for the other person.

Examples:

> *'I was most impressed by the information on your website. You have obviously achieved a good deal of success in a niche market. What took you down that road?'*
>
> *'I've got to leave on the dot of . . . I promised I'd be in for story time. Do you have children?'*
>
> *'We have been thinking of opening an office in the north. I understand you have a base there. Did it take long to get established?'*

Level 5: Maintaining familiarity

Spontaneous sharing and questioning on business or personal matters.

Uses:

- keeping important contacts warm in case business or new connection opportunities should arise
- mutual support and advice
- requesting feedback for yourself
- acquiring testimonials.

Examples:

> *'I was thinking about you last week when I saw the news about. . . How is it going?'*

'What a month! We are sailing too close to the wind at the moment. I think we'll have to find a way of diversifying. I must make some connections in the . . . trade. What do you think?'

'You've known me for a while now. Do you think I'd make it as a lawyer? I've been thinking of doing the conversion course – I am just not happy in my current career.'

Tips for conversing with confidence

Hover hopefully

First you must summon up your Cool Cat Qualities and feel the part. Most of all you need your self-belief. When you enter a room and see everyone engaged in conversation, convince yourself that, however engaged they all seem, at least one of those groups will willingly welcome you into their conversation. If you have time, use a visualisation such as the one given on page 21 to fix a positive image of yourself in your brain. Then give yourself some 'no-nonsense' self-talk and look for a group to start your hovering hopefully by. Our tips on approachable body language in chapter 8, pages 113–14 will help you choose which groups are most open to visitors.

Indicate non-verbally that you are listening and interested (see Listen like a leader, below), and eight times out of ten someone will take the initiative to include you. If they don't, summon up your Resilient Drive (see chapter 4), smile a friendly 'goodbye', and move on positively and purposefully. This is not the time or the place to nurture your emotional wounds (you can do that later!). Tell yourself that you can always try again later if you choose to do so. It is often a good deal easier to do this second time around. People will recognise you and are more likely to automatically invite you in. (This is the subconscious brain up to its tricks again – preferring to be with the familiar.)

As you grow in confidence, you can edge your way into a conversation by using short, non-disruptive interjections to make your presence more noticeable such as: 'How interesting; I agree; that is an amazing statistic; I didn't know that.' Only when you feel comfortable and confident in doing this, should you interrupt with a gem of wisdom or wit. Your nervousness may make this kind of contribution fall flat and kill the flow of the conversation.

Listen like a leader

A recent research project at a leading business school analysed what leaders in the world of work considered to be the key strengths that had contributed to their success. Being a good listener was one that was consistently put at or near the top of their lists. Perhaps you are surprised to read this. Listening is normally considered to be a passive skill and not one that most of us would immediately associate with the movers and shakers in the business world. But the kind of listening that good, confident leaders do is far from passive. It is both active and assertive. It is the kind that ensures that they obtain accurate and relevant information in a short amount of time. Using this style also ensures that they get a quick and true impression of the character and opinions of the person doing the talking.

Nervousness makes minds wander so it is easy for the quality of your listening to plummet if your confidence is low when you are networking. By focusing your attention on using listening techniques like those leaders employ, you can reap even more benefits than a less confident person might. You will lose your self-consciousness and stop worrying about what you are going to say or what the other person is thinking of you or how you can escape as quickly as possible. In addition, you will be perceived as an empathic, alert and endearingly curious person with whom people will enjoy conversing (perhaps because they can continue to do 80 per cent of the talking!).

And furthermore, using our guide below (here is the big bonus!) this can all be achieved in a short space of time. You will no longer have to listen for hours and hours to people who bore you, or can't stay on track or try to overpower you. After you have heard what you need or want to hear you will know how to courteously stop them talking and then buzz on!

Read these tips several times over the next week. But don't rush off and try to use them all at your next event. Instead, first focus on watching confident people when they are listening and see if you can spot these techniques in action (e.g. good TV and radio interviewers, well-trained customer service staff and of course the Big Gun leaders themselves). This will show you how natural and normal the interventions can sound and how effective they are. You can then test each out, one at a time, over the following few weeks. Practise on strangers first, such as people you meet on a train or in the supermarket queue. Or, practise on your family and reap a bonus. You'll find they'll love you even more!

Listen like a leader: a three-phase guide

PHASE 1: Encourage

- Animate your face only.
- Sit or stand in a stable position and lean slightly forward. Putting both feet on the ground usually helps!

- Check that your arms and hands are still. If you are sitting, use one arm to rest your head on. This will keep you focused and indicate that you are going nowhere.
- Open your eyes wide and think 'sparkle' to bring them alive. Aim to maintain eye contact for at least 70 per cent of the time. You can focus on the bridge of the other person's nose, or even their ear if so much eye contact is difficult – they won't notice the difference.
- Move your mouth. Smile, of course, when appropriate, but don't forget there are also other messages that can be conveyed with your mouth, such as surprise and puzzlement. Watch good actors on TV if you don't know what we are talking about!
- Use encouraging and connecting phrases: 'How interesting; what a surprise!'; 'Tell me more . . . and then?'
- Sit on your own 'stories': this is where you will have to work against your brain. It will subconsciously be making connections with what is being said from your own past experiences. So you will feel the urge to come out with a 'That reminds me of . . .' story. Hold these back for now because they will interrupt the other person's flow of thought.
- Replay their final words: this is a technique used by counsellors and journalists. They are often in the position of listening to people who are finding it difficult to talk. It sounds odd until you try it. When the speaker stops, you simply repeat back the last word or two of what they said. This is usually all it takes to prompt them to start again. Trust us – they won't notice you doing it!

PHASE 2: Clarify and connect

- Change posture: this will help you to concentrate better and sends a 'We are moving on' signal. Recent research reveals that changing posture increases our attention span.[3]
- Pick up and check out the feelings: show that you are tuning into them emotionally by picking up on body language clues. For example: 'You sound excited about that prospect' (you heard the voice tone change); 'That must have been difficult' (you saw them frown a little).
- Hazard a guess. Some people are not very expressive, but that doesn't mean that they wouldn't also appreciate emotional recognition. Tentatively explore but be careful not to tell them what they are feeling. For example: 'I was wondering if that worries you.'
- Rewind for more information: if you find that you have lost a particular thread, stop them before you completely lose the plot. It could be that they simply know too much about their own subject and didn't explain fully. But it could be your fault for losing concentration. Don't worry if it was. Stay a Cool Cat and summon up your Unashamed Humility (chapter 6). Stop them talking by gently raising your hand and then back-track to the point where you began to get lost.
- Don't panic in pauses: by now they should be 'in the flow', so trust they are not going to dry up. They may want to catch their breath or just have a brief moment to think. Once again, stay Cool, be still and wait. After about ten seconds you can think about moving it on, but you'll be surprised how rarely you have to do that. Very few people can resist the temptation to talk to an excellent listener.

- Re-phrase in your own words: this is a useful technique to use when you need to clarify your perception of the other person. But it also offers the other person a chance to correct any misperceptions you may have. (It is human nature to hear what we want to hear.) So it should be used even when we know someone quite well.
- Share similar experiences, ideas or feelings: the main purpose of this technique in networking is to start making a connection. But it is good for helping a speaker feel more listened to as well.

PHASE 3: Wind up

- Change posture again: and also this time pull yourself confidently up into a more upright posture while taking a deep breath. This will indicate non-aggressively that you are 'taking charge' of the next phase.
- Change tone and pace: while in listening mode you will probably have automatically been using a lower register than normal. You will probably have been talking more slowly as well. It is now time to quicken up to show that the end is nigh!
- Highlight key points and move on: for example, 'I have been very interested to hear you talk in particular about (a), (b) and (c). What I'd like to move on to discuss now with you, if I may, is . . .'
- Summarise and say goodbye: for example, 'It has been most interesting listening to your experiences. It seems that you have acquired a wealth of knowledge about the East European market, so it could be very useful for us to keep in touch. Do you have a card with you? Here's mine. I must now go and meet some more people. Good luck.'

Don't take your memory for granted

Brain imaging has graphically shown the effect of stress on memory. The memories of big traumas when a high degree of emotion is felt are so deeply embedded into our brain that they may never be forgotten. In contrast, less traumatic stresses, which provoke anxiety rather than a major panic, can inhibit the imprinting of memories. This is why you may not remember names and other important facts you hear when you first meet someone at a networking event or when you are making a difficult phone call to a new contact. Be aware of this and ensure you give your memory a helping hand. Forgetting important information that you know you 'ought' to remember is bad for your self-esteem and won't impress anyone else either.

You will find that many of the Listening like a leader tips we gave you earlier will improve your ability to remember key information, but there are hundreds and hundreds of memory training tricks to try if you haven't already found your own favourites (see Useful websites and Recommended books). But, don't aim to use complicated techniques while networking; you simply don't need them and you often have so little time or concentration power to spare. It is the simple tricks that can become everyday habits that will be most useful. Here are some tricks to try:

- repeating names as often as is appropriate after an introduction and using them again when you say goodbye
- asking how a name is spelt or if it is a diminutive
- making a link in your mind or out loud to another person you know with the same or similar name or telling a link

'story' around it ('I had a very close friend at school who was also called David – he also became an accountant, but we lost contact a while back.'). This is a useful starter to a conversation because it can give the other person a small talk 'peg' to use for their next response (e.g. 'It is so easy to lose contact isn't it? We all seem to lead such busy lives nowadays')

- linking the person's name to a picture in your mind (e.g. to remember David from Wales you could see his name on a flag on top of Snowdonia). Cheryl Buggy, co-author of *Memory Techniques in a Week*, assures us that the sillier the picture, the more effective it is likely to be
- using the person's name on each email you write
- writing a quick reminder on business cards as soon as you can after you have been given a new one. Just a few key words will ensure you recall the person accurately (e.g. 'glasses/golf/trading 5 yrs')
- reading out information or commenting on the business card when you are given it (e.g. 'I see you also have an office in the States – that's interesting')
- mentally adding an adjective to the name of new contacts, noting it in your address book or handheld and then using it each time you think about them or talk to yourself about them. This is particularly helpful when the person has a very common name (e.g. 'I must ring Moustached John tomorrow')
- repeating back key distinguishing information when you say goodbye or when you round off an email (e.g. 'It was good to talk to you John – I hope you have a good trip back to Ipswich')

- making a note of someone's tone of voice or accent when you speak to a new contact on the phone.

If, after trying all these tips, you still forget, try visualising the scene where you first heard the information. Then, mentally re-run the scene and watch yourself in action. This is a very effective way of jogging your memory into action because our brains tend to link words to pictures.

Don't ever be shy about jotting down key information in a small notepad when you are with someone. People will be impressed that you care enough to not take any chances with your memory. Empathy will work in your favour. Hasn't everyone at least one embarrassing story caused by a memory lapse to tell?

Take small talk seriously

We have already mentioned the many uses of small talk and given you a few examples, but it is such a key skill in networking that we want to look at it in more depth. If you are an introvert it is an even more important aspect of conversation for you to work on. You probably hate it! Indeed, this may be one of the main reasons that you find networking so difficult. There is too much of it around. You prefer deeper, more 'meaningful' conversations, and find small talk irritating and superficial.

Both extroverts and introverts can get themselves into difficulties with small talk. In a confidence building or networking workshop we find that introverts usually need to appreciate its function and merit in order to motivate them and then do a good deal of practice so they lose their awkwardness. Extroverts often need to become more aware of when and where it is most appropriate to use it. They often also need to become more skilled at tailoring the subjects to the other person rather than their own interests.

Let's first remind ourselves of why we need small talk. One reason is that it functions as a de-stressor. Believe it or not, even confident people use it for this reason. As long as we are reasonably prepared and skilled at this, it calms us physiologically. Talking about general subjects that trip easily off the tongue and sound familiar have a reassuring effect on our brain, just as sinking into our favourite spot on the sofa does. We feel grounded and safe and more able to be ourselves and be in the here and now. Even if we may not need these benefits ourselves, we cannot assume that those with whom we are talking don't. Many people are very good at covering their inner worries with a mask of composure. If you would prefer them to reveal their true selves, you have to relax them first.

The more relaxed we are the better access we have to our intuition and instincts. These can be invaluable (though not foolproof) when trying to make a judgement about someone. On meeting new people, our bodies automatically set about 'sensing' whether or not this is a person we can trust. A subconscious assessment process goes on which uses body language (and possibly scents) as clues as to whether this person is genuinely OK or not. We then experience the results in terms of a 'gut feeling'. If our minds are preoccupied with complex thoughts or worries, we may not notice these messages from our intuition.

Also, while using only minimal thinking-power to make small talk, we can use our spare cognitive capacity to observe, assess and make mental notes. This will help us to make better decisions about whether this is someone we want to develop a relationship with and if so, what should be our next step. If our intuition, for example, has said a resounding 'no', we can use the small talk as an opportunity to look discreetly around for likely alternatives and think up a polite exit line. We can also use it for this purpose at any time in a conversation should we want to end it or wind it down a level as we indicated in the guide to conversation levels on page 128.

Neutrality is another big advantage of small talk. It enables us to start communicating with people who may be on the opposite end of the value or political scale from us. It may not make us the best of friends, but it does give us a chance to experience each other as fellow human beings. We may find some common ground even if that is only an interest in the weather forecast for the weekend or the seating arrangements for a talk. All experienced negotiators know this start-up 'trick', and it may even have saved the world from a war or two.

Have we convinced you yet? We hope so and we also hope that you give yourself plenty of practise.

Practise your small talk

Before each networking opportunity that you meet, it will help boost your confidence considerably if you have done some preparation. You can't make a connection if you have nothing to talk about. Search out some interesting stories, facts or comparisons before you go to the event. You could for example:

- compare today's weather with that in another country or yesterday's when you were caught out by a downpour
- find out the date the building you are in was constructed or the name of its architect or compare it to another venue about which you have a story to tell
- share some statistics you found on the internet about the host company, topic on the agenda, information on the

background of a contributor or one of the day's big uncontroversial news stories

- when meeting a particular individual, do some prior research on their background or interests. You can do this, for example, by asking questions of the person who put you in contact or looking them up on the internet or company brochure, or chatting to the secretary while you are waiting. You can then use this to ease yourself into the conversation and it shows that you have taken a serious interest in them as a person (e.g. 'John has just told me that you have also worked in Asia for a while – that must have been interesting').

Finally, don't forget to avoid the well-known no-go areas such as politics and religion. They are forbidden territory during small talk for very good reasons. But there are also other subject areas where we recommend that you tread with care. These are the ones that may have a difficult emotional memory or current pain or shame connected to them such as:

- childhood and children
- serious sickness
- bereavement
- weight issues
- age issues
- divorce
- redundancy
- educational background.

You may not yourself have yet stepped into this kind of conversational mine-field, but we can assure you that if you do, and you set off an 'emotional explosion' you won't want to go there again. If you do accidentally stray on to this kind of path, back-track quickly to the safe zone of general subjects or concoct an excuse for a cool-down break by 'needing' a drink, food, the loo or a quick word with a friend. Definitely don't allow the experience to undermine your confidence.

Make music with your voice

You'll be relieved to know that this is not an invitation to literally sing your own praises. It is just a reminder that the quality of your voice matters. It must be easy on the ear. Nervousness plays havoc with voices. It usually makes them go up a tone or two and then they can squeak. It also often robs them of melody. We may talk in a monotone. The volume is also affected. If you are normally on the loud side you could bellow. If you are the softer end, you could be reduced to an inaudible whisper. Unfortunately you are unlikely to spot this effect yourself. So, assume it could happen to you. Then consciously prepare for it because your voice is responsible for 38 per cent of the impression you make with your body language. (The rest of your body contributing 55 per cent, according to the often quoted but controversial research carried out by Professor Albert Mehrabian.)[4]

Remember to breathe more deeply and slowly into your diaphragm. This stops the squeaks and many of the other unpleasing sound effects. Simple upper body stretches and practise before the event or that important phone call will help even more. When you start to speak, remember to vary the volume and the speed at which you talk – and don't be afraid to put in the occasional pause. Just before making your most important point, try this rhythm:

➔ slow down and lower your tone ➔ pause for a moment ➔ discreetly deepen your breathing ➔ make your statement using a lively, upbeat and resonant tone

Then:

- record yourself saying some standard small talk lines
- repeat them until you are satisfied your voice is conveying easy-on-the ear and confident tones. Alternatively, test it out with a straight-talking colleague or friend.

Other ways of improving your voice are to join a drama or singing group. If self-help is not enough, treat yourself to a couple of sessions with a voice coach. They will give you some exercises and tips and loads of supportive encouragement.

Pause before you pose a question

'Questions have more influencing power than statements.'

Hugh Lindsay, *'The Power of the Question', July 2001,* CA Magazine

Take a leaf out of the professional questioner's book and think as long and hard as you can before asking a question. Interviewers, salespeople and researchers know only too well that by doing so you can greatly increase your chance of getting the response you want. We are assuming that you will not misuse this power with questions to get people to say what they would rather not say. The guide below will be a useful tool for easing yourself in and out and through conversations.

Guide to confident questioning

Essentially there are four main types of question. Understanding the role of each can help you make the best of networking opportunities. But beware the 'interrogation'; a Confident Networker is able to skilfully weave probing and prompting questions seamlessly into a conversation.

The four key question types:

1. **Open-ended Questions** are best for initiating a conversation in an uncontroversial and low risk manner. They literally encourage the speaker to 'open up'. They are most effective when starting with 'How?', or 'What?', but can also start with Why?', 'Where?', 'When?' or 'Who?', although the latter are likely to generate a more limited response. They are used to:

- stimulate open communication
- identify common interests
- enable the questioner to 'tune in' to the speaker's mindset and opinions.

> *'Hi I'm Gael. I don't believe we've met before. What brings you to this evening's special event?'*
>
> *'Hi I'm Stuart. It's great to see this event so well attended. How do you know the host?'*

2. **Reflective Questions** are best for developing rapport and showing respect and interest. As pointed out earlier in Listen like a leader – Phase 1: Encourage (page 134), one form of reflective questioning is simply replaying the speaker's last few words, which provides encouragement for them to keep going. They are also useful for clarifying or probing more deeply into the topic under discussion. A well-constructed Reflective Question (RQ) summarises or paraphrases and reflects back

what has just been said. It is most effective if at least some words are changed. A parrot-like response can seem overly contrived and therefore insincere, unless you're simply prompting them to continue. They are used to:

- indicate you are keen to listen to and understand what has been said, thereby demonstrating empathy
- allow emphasis on the points of agreement/common interests on which you would like to build
- keep the speaker on track
- generate a 'that's right' agreement or elicit a more in-depth response about a topic of interest.

'Although we're all very busy at the moment, I'm pleased that this briefing has been extended to include the possible implications of the new legislation that will soon confront us.'

RQ 'So you're happy that the likely impacts on the industry of the new legislation are going to be covered at this event?'

'It's crucial I attend the workshop part of this conference today.'

RQ 'Oh, it's crucial is it? Why is that particularly important for you?'

3. Directive (or Closed) Questions are best for gaining quick confirmation of facts. They demand a simple 'Yes' or No' or limited response. They can take the form of Leading Questions. These are really statements made to 'appear' like questions with the addition of words such as 'isn't it?' or don't we?' They are used to:

- shift power back to the questioner
- test commitment
- finalise an arrangement
- close the conversation.

Beware of moving too quickly into this directive questioning mode. This is a common mistake. Before you use these types of questions you should have established areas of common interest or have built a good level of rapport. Unless you have, these questions will have you marked as either uninterested, pushy or arrogant. However, used with care, they are a very powerful tool for gaining agreement and moving on:

'So we're both happy that we progress our discussions along these lines?'

But this obviously pre-supposes that the questioner had established this agreement before popping the question.

The following 'innocent' sounding Directive Questions could therefore receive either short shrift or a positive response, dependent on what pattern of questioning, responses and establishment of rapport has preceded them.

'So you'll accept my invitation to speak at next week's event?'

'Are you a regular contributor to this cause?'

'Would any of your colleagues be interested in this idea, do you think?'

4. Hypothetical Questions allow for safely 'testing the water' to help further clarify interests and intentions, prior to any commitment. They usually take the form of 'What if ...?' questions. They are used to:

- minimise any sense of 'pressure' by requesting their reaction to an (as yet) fictional or potential situation
- summarise points of agreement, and explore ways of overcoming possible blockages in a non-threatening manner.

A well-designed Hypothetical Question enables the speaker to respond more dispassionately and objectively, thereby making it more likely the questioner will learn more about their genuine focus and concerns. This in turn increases the chances of mutually beneficial networking opportunities. For example:

> *'How would you feel if . . .?'*
>
> *'Another accountant I know says . . . what do you think of that?'*
>
> *'If you had the opportunity to . . . what would you do?'*

These are great questions to use when you have reached the Polite Probing stage of a conversation (remember page 130).

Deflect or bounce back unwelcome questions

You've probably seen many a politician do this on TV and maybe you have found it intensely irritating. That is because it works – it gets them off the hook and they don't have to reveal what they want to conceal.

But, because someone else misuses this technique don't dismiss it yourself. You may need it especially while you are still building up your confidence or haven't established enough trust as yet in your questioner. Remember, not every networker is a skilled conversationalist (or mind reader!) and may not realise they have posed an overly 'pushy' or personal question. When someone poses a question they are placing the ball in your court and what you then do with it is your responsibility. The minute you sense the uncomfortable feeling that an awkward question generates, pause, take a deep breath and respond politely and calmly with a deflector and/or bounce the ball back with another question or subject as in these examples:

'You seem too young to be in charge of a ward. How old are you?'

➔ 'Things aren't always what they seem. I wonder why my age should interest you. Do you have a lot of direct contact with hospital staff in your role?'

'So what do they pay senior accountants in a firm like yours nowadays?'

➔ 'That depends on many variables. What makes you ask? Are you thinking of changing careers?'

'Can we fix a date for me to come and show you what we do?'

➔ 'I'd like to think about that. I have your card. You were telling me earlier that you have been here before. Were there as many people here then?'

Prepare a commercial cross-over script

Now this is one of the most crucial conversations of them all!

Much of the time when we are networking in the world of work, our conversations feel more social than businesslike. But at some point in the proceedings we have to take the bull by the horns and go for what we really came for – trade. You may be networking to sell your skills and know-how, or a particular product or service. Alternatively, you may be doing it to buy, recruit or find out more about the competition or a particular market. The nature of your trade may vary. Sometimes it might be straightforwardly financial, or it could be an exchange of favours, skills or valuable contacts.

How often do you put off making that dreaded cross-over from friendly chit-chat into a serious business conversation? How much time are you wasting waiting for that 'ideal moment' or for the other person to do the hard transition work for you?

'Too often' and 'Too much' we guess might be your answers. We understand the difficulty. It is hard for anyone to start making a 'pitch' when networking. It is so much easier to do when you are in a more obvious commercial context such as a trade fair or a job interview. So no wonder unconfident people often find this an impossible challenge unless they are extremely well prepared before taking the plunge.

We believe that one of the best ways of preparing yourself psychologically is to compose and rehearse a script. We have designed a formula for doing this, which we call a Commercial Cross-over Script. As we said earlier, although the specific outcome you may want from this development in your relationship may not involve a direct exchange of money, indirectly it will have a kind of commercial element. This script can therefore be used to make any conversational transition from a networking relationship to one where your business or career could be advanced.

Please remember that once you have moved the relationship into the commercial arena, you are no longer networking and it is over to you! Helping you to 'sell' yourself, an idea, a service or a product is not within the scope of this book! But there are, of course, plenty of other books around on this subject.

Compose your script along the lines we outline below. The framework has been carefully designed to hook the other person's interest and empathy so that they will not feel they are being 'threatened' with a pushy 'sales pitch'. So spend as much time as you can on its composition. You might find it helpful to re-read our guide to confident language first (pages 156–9).

Aim to make your script sound concise, punchy and natural. The more you edit the better. Do the key sentences first. Then read it out loud and add or change filler and link phrases to make it run smoothly. It should sound conversational in tone and not like the start of a formal presentation. When you are satisfied that it is good enough (not perfect!), practise saying it in front of the mirror or to a supportive friend or colleague. And, don't forget to use non-verbal confident body language as you are doing so (pages 160–1).

Also, take a look at what Andy Lopata, managing director of BRE Networking has to say:

> *'People buy people. People mainly buy passion – if you are not passionate about your business, why should anyone else be? Whatever your doubts, leave them behind when you are talking with others and be positive and passionate. For networking to be successful, we need to inspire others to want to connect with us, and that comes from self-evident self-belief.*

Commercial cross-over scripts: outline and example

1. Value the relationship

This is a positive way to start and should establish a friendly climate. (Of course it will only do so if you really do have a good relationship, but then if you didn't, you shouldn't be writing this script at all!)

> 'We have known each other now for about three months. I have really enjoyed your company and our chats about Man United's sad demise in particular!'

2. Highlight noticed need and possible appeal

It is important to show that you have listened to them and that you are responding to their expressed interest or need and not just doing a speculative sell.

> *'I know we haven't talked very much about business, but I did notice that you have several times mentioned an interest in the Asian market, which, as you know, is where 50 per cent of our operations are now based.'*

3. Acknowledge and ease discomfort

Remember the other person may find the cross-over as awkward as you do. If you indicate that you have thought about their feelings as well, they are more likely to be receptive.

> *'I appreciate that you may not feel comfortable talking about business here.'*

4. Make direct request

Don't beat about the bush – get to the point quickly.

> *'I'd like to have an opportunity to tell you more about what we do and our plans for expansion.'*

5. Suggest mutual pay-off

Networking aims to be a win/win activity. Make it clear that you would want a mutually beneficial outcome to result from any cross-over into a commercial or career advancement relationship.

> 'I believe that there may be ways we could both benefit from developing some kind of commercial partnership.'

6. Close with multiple choice question

This will (a) test their interest (as in classic sales pitches) and (b) give them an easy escape route (not a feature of most classic sales pitches!). If you are used to using this kind of question in the classic sales way, be aware of the difference. Your objective in this context is to whet their appetite for a business opportunity, but not at the expense of your networking relationship. We strongly advise you to take the risk of giving them an escape route option. If enough trust has been established through networking, and there is a business opportunity to be had, the other party will bite. If they don't do it now, they will later. Never push your luck with a 'cornering' sales technique in networking. It will damage your reputation and weaken your connection to the network.

> *'Would you like me to send you some information and set up a meeting or would you prefer that I didn't?'*

A visualisation exercise to programme your brain to expect a positive outcome

The night before you think you may deliver your script, use a visualisation such as the one below to programme your brain to expect a positive outcome when you use your script.

Exercise

Use a warm aromatic bath or your favourite relaxation exercise to put your body into a deeply relaxed state (e.g. tensing and slowly releasing each muscle in your body – one by one in time with slow deep breathing).

Close your eyes and take a few more slow breaths while allowing your body to 'melt into' whatever surface is currently supporting it. (You could imagine you are lying on warm soft sand or even a very large tub of butter!)

Run a mental movie through your mind (in glorious digital colour and sound, don't forget!). Use your imagination to watch and hear yourself delivering your script in a highly confident manner to several different people and notice their expressions as they respond with enthusiastic interest.

Repeat three times.

Finally, remember that even if you don't eventually use your prepared script word for word, it will have built your confidence. You will certainly find the cross-over much easier because you will be more articulate and composed and have more appeal.

Guide to confident language

Here are some examples of the types of words and phrases used by confident people:

Big picture thinking	'The vision I have in mind is …'; 'In five years I expect to …'; 'My dream is that we will …'; 'What is your overall objective?'; 'The end result of that kind of policy/ outlook will be …'; 'I'd like to see them focus more on permanent solutions rather than the short-term alleviation of the symptoms …'; 'It's important to consider the wider perspective, don't you think …'
Ethical and principle centred	'I believe …'; 'I always ensure that …'; 'We always put a high value on …'; 'a quality of which we are justly proud'; 'I think they should take a stand on …'; 'let's not forget that their mission is supposed to be …'; 'the guiding principle behind this project …'
Learned	'According to the latest research (quote source) …'; 'In a recent article in (quote publication) ….; I was reading an interesting blog discussion on this (quote weblink) …'; 'Is this the most up-to-date version?'; 'What new measures have been taken …'; 'Perhaps a more innovative approach is called for …'; 'In the future we will …'; 'Having looked at the evidence, I think …'
Diagnostic	'Over the last few months, the trend in the economy has been … this shows, I believe, that ….'; 'the underlying problem appears to be …'; 'the heart of the matter is …'
Taking responsibility	'The buck had to stop somewhere, so I decided to …'; 'Let's find a way …'; 'It's a tough world out there, but let's think what we can do to …'; 'Something appears to be not quite right, I'll investigate …'; 'I have forgotten your name, I am so sorry …'
Proactive	'I have heard so much about you that I would like to introduce myself'; 'We are no longer given the opportunity to pass the time of day with

	colleagues, so I am tabling a motion …'; 'I decided to join because I wanted to extend my contacts'; 'I couldn't afford to wait for … so I …'; 'there was no point in worrying, so instead I …'
Positive	'I am sure there will be a way for us …'; 'I am looking forward to …'; 'I trust …'; 'the possible advantages are …'
Clear priority and direction	'With limited resources, we have to ensure …'; 'Our critical tasks are …'; 'We must all understand and agree a step-by-step plan before …'; 'What is your key objective here?'; 'This needs urgent attention …'; 'This good result indicates that in the future we should consider …'
Decisive	'We need to decide now in spite of …'; 'We could always make use of more information but …' ; 'It's a risk we'll have to take …'; 'Have you made up your mind? Count me in!'
Constructively challenging	'Is that the only option?'; 'Maybe there's a better way'; 'An alternative way of looking at it might be …'; 'But let's suppose that …'; 'If I were to take the Devil's advocate position I might say that …'; 'I don't agree because …'
Direct	'I don't want to beat about the bush, I would like to ….'; 'I want to get straight to the point …'; 'Are you really saying that … because if that is so, we must …'; 'We can't afford to wait any longer, so …'; 'What do you think about …?'
Inspirational and motivational	'We can do this – I know you have both the knowledge and skills'; 'I am sure you'll find it very satisfying'; 'We will all feel well rewarded if …'; 'Won't you be proud of such an achievement?'
Emotional, but moderated by rationality	'I feel really excited about this opportunity and after studying the evidence we'; 'I'm not at all happy about the progress of … so I would suggest

	that we study the statistics before ...' ; 'my gut feeling about this is ... but I would like to hear more about your experiences in the field'
Co-operative	'Let's pool our thoughts on ...'; 'if we exchanged a few contacts together we could ...'; 'as a team of ...'; 'before talking further, it may help if we both exchanged our last three annual reports'; 'Let's see if we can find a mutually beneficial way of pooling our talents and resources ...'; 'Let's work out how we can best collaborate to integrate our knowledge to ...'
Proud	'My biggest achievement to date has been ...'; 'I am pleased with the way I ...'; 'It was difficult for me to come today, I prefer small gatherings. But I did and I succeeded in making some great contacts'
Humble	'It took me many mistakes before I succeeded in ...'; 'That's not my field, I'd welcome some enlightenment on that subject'; 'One of my bad habits is ...'; 'I always need help with ...'; 'I don't understand that point, could you explain in more detail'

Useful confident-sounding sentence fillers

Certainly	Of course
Obviously	In my opinion
Clearly	There's no denying that ...
Naturally	There's no question that it was ...

Language to avoid or use with care

- Acronyms: define them or ditch them
- Generalities: convert these to specifics

- Exaggerations: convert to data (even if rough figures) whenever possible
- Effusive emotional words
- Cynical comments
- Swear words
- Clichés
- Highly hip or dated expressions
- Weak fillers: um; ah
- Self-put-downs: such as 'It's only me'; 'I'm not much of …'; 'What an idiot I looked'; 'Compared to yours my card is so dull'
- Inducing criticism: such as 'You'll probably think this is a crazy idea'; 'You may not rate my experience but …'
- Over-apologetic: 'I can't tell you how sorry I am, it was a terrible thing to do to miss the bus. I am so dreadfully sorry. What must you think of me? Will you ever forgive me?' instead of 'I am sorry to have let you down by arriving late. Can I buy you a drink as recompense?'

Confident body language

- Facial expression: relaxed brow, smiling as appropriate
- Eyes: alert but not staring; using direct eye contact as often as the culture permits (60 to 70 per cent of the time in most European cultures)
- Stance: shoulders down and back; diaphragm pulled up and

abdominals in and back; feet slightly apart; no crossed limbs; neck elongated and head pulled upright

- Personal space: keeping your distance appropriate (e.g. in UK business culture this would be no closer than 60 cm)
- Sitting position: relaxed and open; upright or leaning slightly forward and head slightly tilted when listening; hands unclasped and held loosely on lap or on table; legs uncrossed with both feet on the floor
- Walk: even, firm, purposeful but relaxed and unhurried steps
- Voice: good projection, lively and varied tone
- Gestures: expressive but controlled and purposefully reinforcing verbal message; non-fidgety; never putting your hand over your face.

10

E-connect with magnetism

IN THE LAST SIX OR seven years, as a result of increasing access to the internet, there has been an explosion of new networking opportunities. These are often referred to as e-networking. You may already use one or two of the methods available. For example, you can use email to develop and maintain new relationships; you can 'meet' potential new contacts by participating in discussion forums (usually referred to as blogging) on special interest websites; you can use instant messaging such as MSN for on-line conversations and meetings. You can also meet people by joining on-line business and social networks specifically set up to help people find jobs, staff, business partners, experts and others they might want to meet.

The internet has also opened up opportunities in terms of making an impact. You can make yourself and what you can provide visible to a much broader community than would ever be possible face-to-face. For example, by putting your profile on a professional, company or association website or creating your own business website, you can now meet people in almost every corner of the world that has access to the web.

Are you sure that you are making the most of e-networking? In the privacy of your home or office, you can meet people of any age and any background and in any business at the click of a few computer buttons. (We are assured that we are a maximum of only 19 clicks away from anyone in the web world.) And, if your eventual aim is to meet people face-to-face (as it usually is), you can build the foundations of a relationship before your first real-life encounter. This means that the disabling 'fear of the unknown' factor is greatly reduced. So too is that equally disabling factor – the inferiority complex. Because e-connecting strips away that distancing 'halo' effect from people with big personalities and stunning looks, it feels much less intimidating to approach people whom you might otherwise run a mile from.

Even people whose confidence is high often find e-networking a good deal less stressful as well. Most people we have spoken to say they find it a hundred times easier to initiate a 'conversation' with anyone through email than through meeting them at social events or having to pick up the phone and make a 'cold call'. They also say that they find it easier as well as quicker to make an impressive virtual impact. When you don't have to worry about what to wear, what to say, how to make a charismatic entrance or how to respond to awkward questions, you can concentrate better on making your message about your services and specialisms clear, precise and visually appealing.

We have now been actively involved in the e-networking world for a number of years and have seen how it has created opportunities that would otherwise not have emerged. Here are just a few of the typical success stories that we have encountered:

CASE STUDY

A human resources professional who had just been made redundant posted her profile on a business networking site and was asked to attend a job interview within 24 hours. She was thrilled to accept this ideal job, which she told us she could never have found through traditional recruitment channels or through her existing network of contacts.

An entrepreneur joined an on-line business network, which within one year had provided him with new business that represented 75 per cent of his total revenue.

An expert in the field of sustainable development, by learning how to e-network with more impact, increased his total number of contacts from around 200 to over 4,000 within nine months. This enabled him to have a more influential voice in the corridors of ecological power.

In one of the on-line UK business networks we belong to, two members have recently started a 'House of Commons club'. The club hosts on-line discussions and organises monthly lunches, which offer their members a chance to lunch with a senior figure from Parliament.

We are sure that you too will have much to gain from e-connecting if you don't already. But nevertheless, it could still present difficulties that you may not be prepared for. This is an extract from an email we received last year and illustrates how many people feel on starting this kind of networking.

'The first thing I found difficult was how exposed you feel when you join an on-line network. I instantly received

> *messages from people I had never met or heard of before, who had spotted that I had just joined. It felt as though I had publicly announced my presence in some way, instead of just sneaking in to have a look around (my preferred style in a new environment). It can be quite daunting if you are unused to that level of visibility!'*
>
> Louise, *an on-line networker*

Despite this initial reticence, Louise is now a staunch supporter of this way of networking and now has many success stories to tell.

False security

One cause of common problems is that e-networking can give you a false sense of security. Even though you are not being seen or may be visible only from a carefully selected photo, you still can appear weak, wimpish, boring and unprofessional. You can also still feel overly daunted by people's impressive e-profiles, elaborate websites, prolific connections and IT savvy, and therefore play the field too safely. We would hazard a fairly informed guess that among the millions who only stay a short while in e-networks, a fair proportion of these suffer with low confidence. The 'culture' of the e-world can feel alienating to anyone whose self-belief and self-protective skills are shaky.

What is it about this culture that you may find difficult? The primary challenge is that the internet is a super-fast-paced global world where easy-going informality masks intense competitiveness. The sheer size of the group we find ourselves in encourages aggression. (It is a well-proven sociological phenomenon that the larger the group, the more likely aggression within it will be, and the more contagious it becomes as well.) So also does the fact that there are no tangible reminders of the humanness of the contacts that are made. Again research and many people's bitter experience of war and prison has shown that the more dehumanised a person is, the easier it is to behave aggressively with them. On the net, you may appear to some people to be a very dispensable speck in an overpopulated universe. As a result, you are almost guaranteed to meet some unfriendly and even outright 'nasty' behaviour. Electronic messages are often written impulsively and quickly and can therefore be overly blunt and curt. Web discussions have a tendency to escalate very quickly into arguments that use strong language and negative labelling. You may hear these kinds of behaviours referred to as 'flaming' by e-networkers.

But don't be frightened off! Reputable business networks such as those we will introduce you to in Wise Owl Know-how, chapter 14 are actively trying to deal with these problems. We know that they are doing their utmost to establish 'netiquette' codes and exclude those who break these. Increasingly, many are encouraging the use of photos, which, although having some disadvantages, certainly helps to humanise interactions. But essentially, it is an unprotected environment where dog eats dog daily.

Your best defence is undoubtedly inner confidence. A very close second best is taking the advice we have gathered for you below, which will increase your outer confidence internet skills. Our tips have been compiled in consultation with a range of internet experts. In doing so, we have assumed that most people reading this book will have some basic computer literacy and have access to email and the internet. If you do not have these, we strongly recommend that you acquire them as soon as you can. Not only will you miss out on the network revolution, but nowadays, even in the face-to-face networking world, you will discover that people use the internet extensively as an additional means of connecting.

We believe that this advice will help you to stay cool and buzz around the net in spite of its scary aspects. It will ensure that you feel more competent, have high visibility and stand out among the crowd while still reflecting the real you that they would meet face to face. As e-connecting can become even more powerful when used with other forms of non-face-to-face communication, we have also included some tips on how to make the most of networking in the telephonic and snail mail hives.

Tips for e-connecting with magnetism

Take image factors very seriously

First impressions are just as important when networking electronically as they are face to face. In fact they may be even more important, because if someone doesn't instantly respond positively to our e-presence in, for example, an email, weblog or web profile, they will make their decision even faster and may dismiss you forever there and then. In real life they may, for reasons of politeness or kindness, at least hear you out. Then, if they haven't taken an instant dislike, most will usually give you a second chance.

The means by which we present our image are different when we are operating electronically. We do not have the body language or clothes factors to help or hinder us. But 'looks' are nevertheless very important. Before setting off to network face to face, we would probably give some prior thought to how we will present ourselves and will adapt our style according to whom we think we will meet. Most people don't do this when working electronically; they use the same style of writing and the same 'look' for the way they present their messages to everyone.

So, as well as taking on board the advice in the next two tips, remember those we gave in chapter 8 Impact instantly. Much of it is still applicable in the electronic world. Certainly, you need to check that the image you are conveying fits with your three adjectives and is appropriate for the audience with whom you are communicating. And don't forget that the actual words you use to create your first impression are even more important in this medium than they are face to face. They have to work so much harder because there are no smiles, tones of voice or posture cues to help convey your humanness and empathy. Even the words used in your email address or website name can be make-or-break image factors. We know, for example, that applications for jobs from people with 'jokey' email or web addresses are often not even read or looked at. We can assume that the same kinds of judgements are being made during networking as well.

Write emails that will be opened and read

The growth in email is startling. It's estimated that current volumes are topping 30 billion per day, that's a three-fold increase in just four years (*Fortune Technology Trends Report*, January 2005). Busy people (and they are probably the ones you want to connect with) often dread opening their in-boxes especially after a day or two away from their computer. The sheer volume of correspondence puts them in a negative mood to start with, so the first challenge is to get read. The second is to make them want to respond – quickly. (If an email isn't responded to within a day or two of receipt, it often gets overlooked.) These guidelines will help you to be seen and create the impression that you deserve a response!

Guidelines for emails

- **Stick to the 'one subject, one email' rule.** It is tempting to fire off an email to an individual with the two or three things that are on your mind. But this rule makes it easier for the recipient to scan the subject lines and see what you want, rather than being presented with an email titled just 'Hi'. It also makes it easier to prioritise what you may have asked them to do or consider. They can give an immediate response to some and flag the ones that need a more thought-through reply.
- **Make the heading eye-catching but appropriate.** Witty words may draw attention, but are they a good way to convey a serious professional image? It is more important to ensure that the heading bears some relationship to the subject matter. This often does not happen – especially if you press the reply button and have not bothered to change the heading as the discussion develops between you. Appropriate headings also make it easier for people to track down a particular email by using the 'Find' tool.
- **Use the person's name** even when you start an email informally without a formal 'Dear . . .'. Start instead with, for example, 'Hi Gael . . .' or 'That's great news Stuart'. This helps humanise the contact and is good for your memory!
- **In an on-going electronic discussion, lead the reader into the email by back-tracking** with a few reminders. This will save them having to wade through the old correspondence and they will be grateful and much more likely to respond quickly.

- **Start with a summary** – busy people are often skim readers and may not go beyond the first paragraph.
- **Use plain English** – but keep your tone polite and not too informal until you have received several emails from your contact and know that that is how they like to operate. The golden rule for email writing is 'If you wouldn't say it, don't write it.' Your email 'voice' should sound alive and convey some feeling. In informal exchanges people now often use symbols referred to as emoticons to convey for example a smile ☺ or concern ☹. Try to avoid using an impersonal third person voice. For example, use 'I think that we could . . .' instead of 'It would appear that it is best to . . .'
- **Keep your sentences and paragraphs short.** The convention is for them to be much shorter than you would find in other business or professional documents. Sentences should be no more than 35 words long and paragraphs broken up or formatted with bullet points. If your subject matter deserves more explanation, put it into a document and attach it. The whole email should not be longer than one screen. So edit, edit and edit!
- **Use simple formatting** – what looks impressive on your screen may look a mess on that of someone else if their email programme is different. As a general rule, don't use the caps lock button – capitalising is called 'SHOUTING' and is considered very bad netiquette (manners).
- **Be direct** – state clearly what action you want your reader to take. Once Gael has established a relationship, she often fronts her questions with a series of question marks. This trick greatly increases the chances of getting her important questions answered.
- **Sign off** – with good wishes, your name and a formal signature. The latter is your on-line business card. Include a link to your

website or your on-line profile on another site, but only include your telephone numbers if you are sure that you don't mind that person calling you. Most people now also include an edited-down version of their elevator pitch, or their company mission statement and their logo if they have one. As you become surer of yourself and your image, you could add a favourite quote or saying or a 'news flash' to your signature. This is a way of stamping your personality on the email and sharing something about your values, your business and making yourself more memorable.

- **Check your email before sending it** – always use the spell checker. If your email programme doesn't have one, compose long sections of text first in a Word document and then paste it in once it has been checked.
- **Don't overuse the 'high priority' or 'request receipt' tools** on every email. It is an annoying habit.
- **Beware the dangers of 'Blast-mailing'** – certainly don't send out information emails too often. This makes more enemies than friends. You'll be directed into the spam file fast! Who doesn't suffer from information overload nowadays? When you do send out the same information email to a number of people (using cut and paste) do remember to delete the previous person's name and company and any appropriate inclusions and exclusions you added. If you have ever received an email where this hasn't been done, you probably pressed the delete button pretty fast.

Perch your confident profile on ready-made web habitats

The more websites on which you are featured the more chance you have of making new connections. The on-line networks are obvious places; alternatively there are professional associations and clubs that you could feature your profile on. If you work for a company, you may of course have a profile on their site. In Wise Owl Know-how you will find many suggestions on how to find such places.

When composing your profile to place on a site make sure that it appears confident and appealing to others. It needs to clearly state your special skills and interests; how you can help others and any specific kinds of people whom you are looking to meet (e.g. someone with the same work interests or someone who is an investor or might be able to connect you to new staff). Begin with a concise summary that has impact. The elevator pitch you composed earlier (chapter 8) can be slightly adapted and stretched for this purpose.

Take great care when choosing a photo to accompany your profile. You should look relaxed, energised and warm but also professional. Your eyes should be clearly visible and will need to look bright and sparkling in order to leap off the screen. All this is hard to achieve. Sometimes going to a professional photographer for these kinds of photos is not a good idea. For people who are camera shy, they often produce results that are too 'formal' for networking profiles on the internet. You may be better entrusting this task to a friend with a digital camera and go to a location where you can feel relaxed and will give a real-life background interest to the picture as well. Take about 50 shots and there is sure to be a winner. But get help choosing the best one. You may not be the best person to make this choice!

Get into action that has e-visibility

Later we will be looking at many ways to build up your reputation. But nowadays ensuring that you have a good presence on the internet is the most important of all. If someone wants to find out more about you, the first action they will nowadays take is to type your name into an internet search engine. (A leading headhunting firm recently told Stuart that they check every candidate's 'presence' on the internet. This constitutes their 'first impression', and can enhance or limit their employment opportunities.) Generally speaking, the more matches anyone finds, the more impressed they will be. But those matches must take them to data that will impress them even more. So it is good to do checks every so often yourself on what the search engines are turning up. It is all about using key words in the right way and it could be well worth consulting an expert on how to do this.

But, of course, first there has to be the right kind of data for the key words to find. This is your job! Make sure that you are doing the following kinds of activities and that they are regularly being featured on the web in some form or other:

- Writing: weblogs (see tip below), newsletters, lists of helpful tips, articles and even books
- Talking: at conferences and public meetings which are going to be flagged up on the net
- Leading: chairing or organising meetings and public events or running workshops and courses
- Giving: of your time to community and charity events and working parties for change
- Getting quoted: in the media on your specialist subject, in particular.

Know your netiquette

We cannot stress enough the importance of netiquette or good manners on the internet. If you don't play by its rules, you will stand very little chance of making good connections. Look again at Ecademy's code of ethics in chapter 3 Incorruptible integrity, pages 54–5. Before you join any other group, check out whether they too have a code.

Blog with impact

For those of you who are not yet acquainted with blogging, blog is short for weblog. This is a web page that serves as a publicly accessible personal journal for an individual. However, in the last few years many companies, e-networks and clubs now have their own discussion forums where blogs can be posted. Originally it was a way of storing and sharing, commenting quickly and informally on links to web pages where the bloggers found interesting information. Good forums are now highly interactive. They are typically updated daily but an international business network forum can generate hundreds of blogs per hour.

Blogging is now considered so influential that many people in the e-networking field are saying that we should make a rule to do a blog a day if we want to make an impact and remain competitive. As we write, the magazine *Business Week* has just published yet another article on the blogging phenomenon. It stresses the importance of writing them whether you like it or not.

> *'Go ahead and bellyache about blogs – but don't close your eyes. They're the most explosive outbreak in the information*

> *world since the internet itself. Blogs will shake up just about every business – including yours. Whether you ship paper clips or pork bellies you cannot ignore, postpone or delegate them. Given the changes barrelling down, blogs aren't a business elective: they're a prerequisite.'*
>
> *Business Week*, April 2005

But we believe that there is a good way of blogging and a not so good way. You can make a negative impact by just using it to 'sound off'. So we consulted Allan Engelhardt, an internet expert and the founder of Cybaea, a web strategy business, for his views on writing blogs that will get you noticed in the right way. This is what he said:

> *'There are over 800 new blog posts every minute. It is a competitive market. If you want to be in it, then you must find your subject niche as well as your voice.*
>
> *'Your voice is important. There will always be somebody out there who writes about the same things as you. But you have a unique perspective. You have lived a unique life, met a unique collection of people and experienced a unique set of events. Your perspective on the things you care about is important.*
>
> *'If you want to be found by the search engines, focus.*
>
> *'If you want to be found by people, then focus is also required. Simply: if you have attracted someone to your site because of a subject you covered, then they are only going to come back to you if you write more on the same topic that interests them. If they are into blue flowers but you write about your cat for the next three months, then they will give*

up trying to follow your writings. (Unless they also have a feline fetish.)

'Do not be afraid to show your passion. Your on-line presence can be the thing that makes you explore your interests deeper because you are sharing it with strangers.'

We would like to add these three extra tips. They were gleaned from a recent weblog discussion on one of the networks to which we belong:

- make sure the content of your blog is longer than the signature that goes underneath it. Refrain from annoying one-liners
- be inclusive – no in-jokes with your chums
- remember the 15-second attention span rule applies.

You will find more information on the blogging phenomenon in Wise Owl Know-how, chapter 17, pages 255–6.

Make your e-chat enticing

There are now many ways to engage in discussions on the net. There are chat rooms, weblogs and forums on most big sites, and most networking platforms will have them. The more you participate in these the better. The best of them are linked to Google. Much of the advice we gave earlier on emailing is applicable. Keep your language plain, concise, lively and, of course, polite. Don't engage in making direct sales pushes, but do refer to what you have to offer others. Try to slip into your chat information that could be helpful to others and will show that you are competent, well read and up to date. For example, you could write a blog or message for your forum group about a piece of news or a research finding that could be of interest and start a discussion around this subject. Remember, however, that the object of the exercise is not to lecture or sermonise, but to engage people in a discussion. So ask open questions that will prompt this kind of reply (remember our earlier advice on this topic in chapter 9, page 146) and choose subjects that will 'tease' people into responding.

Create a cool-looking website

Those of you who are sole traders or have small businesses will almost certainly benefit from having your own website. If you have enough technology-savvy, you could quite easily create your own. Or, if not, it is relatively inexpensive to have a specialist do this for you. The same provider can also probably advise you on how to generate 'page impressions' and 'visitors' to increase visibility for your site using so-called 'web search engine optimisation' techniques.

For business networking, it is important that any website you have looks professional and is easy to use. The following guidelines were written for us by Simon Graham, a web designer and partner at a web design agency, and an ace e-networker himself.

Guidelines on creating a confident-looking website

- Keep it clean – don't use hundreds of different colours, animations and font styles – and you will make a much better impression. Stick to one font face (Arial and Verdana are perfect for screen reading) and only vary its size and colour for titles and regular/bold text.
- Keep the navigation simple; don't have navigation options all over the place; make sure your site is easy to use.

Having the main menu across the top or down the left, with information pages such as terms and conditions in the footer, will work just fine.

- Avoid cheesy photos. Too many business websites show people in a meeting or two people in suits shaking hands. Excite your visitors, don't send them to sleep!
- Your logo should work at all sizes – when designing your logo, think about all the places it will be used. The logo may look great when large on your website or on a poster, but this will not be so good if it becomes unreadable when you shrink it down for use on a business card.
- Don't use free web hosting – a 'host' is the place where your website lives on the internet. If you want to know more, type – define: Web Host – into Google and do a search. Free hosting companies such as 'Yahoo! Geocities' will add unrelated adverts to your website (which is why they are free), undermining all your hard work.
- HTML and design – if you are new to websites and are going to build the site yourself, you are going to have to get your hands dirty and learn some basic coding and how to use web design packages such as Dreamweaver, FrontPage, Fireworks and Photoshop. http://www.htmlgoodies.com/ is one of the best websites to start learning HTML code and there are plenty of books on this topic.
- Make the site search engine friendly – as well as looking great, people must be able to find you on the major search engines (websites such as Google or Yahoo!). Check out http://www.searchenginewatch.com – this site has plenty of free information about this topic.
- Use your name on every page – if you are a consultant/small business, it is unlikely people will find

you by searching for a 'Business Development Consultant' on Google, they will want to find you by either using your name or your company name after meeting you at a networking event.

- Look like an expert – add some papers or articles and this will give you authority. Another alternative is to add testimonials or case studies from real clients. This content will also help you appear in search engine results as it will help them work out who you are and what you do.
- Write concisely for screen reading – people will not want to read your life story on screen. After a slow site, nothing makes someone go back to Google quicker than a long, boring page. Don't use 10,000 words when 200 will do the job!
- Only have a news section if you will update it regularly – nothing makes you look lazier than a news section that was last updated on 25 April 1995!
- Have a press section – if you want to try and make it into the press, make it easy for journalists to find out about you by adding a press section. A good example can be seen at http://www.marketpublic.com/press.php
- Be legal – websites should have both privacy policies and terms of use. It is also best practice to include a copyright statement. Get your solicitor to give a fixed price up front. Having these sections not only offers you more protection; it also makes you appear more professional.
- Don't hide your contact details – make it easy for people to get in touch by either having your contact details on every page or in a clearly defined 'Contact us' section.

Stay focused approximately 80 per cent of your time

The web can be a great time waster as well as a time saver and a great place to find new connections. So set yourself time limits for random surfing. Keep your network strategy (with its priority points brightly highlighted) pinned up beside your computer to remind you to keep to task at least most of the time.

When and how to pick up the phone instead

Diane Darling, a top networking guru from the USA and author of *The Networking Survival Guide*, has this interesting tip for 2005 on her website: 'Go low tech – pick up the phone instead of emailing.'

The overwhelming bulk of your non-face-to-face networking will inevitably be on the net nowadays, but you can add another dimension to your relationship by picking up the phone and talking. This used to be impossibly expensive, especially if you needed to network internationally, but now there are ways and means of making calls via the web for a very low price. The big advantage of doing this is that if you have a web camera you can see each other as well. At the time of writing, the technology is relatively new and the lines and pictures can be a bit fuzzy, but things are rapidly improving as technology advances.

You could set aside a specific time in your diary once a month for making random 'Hello calls' and this will make sure that they happen. But also use the telephone if you can whenever there are issues involving feelings to deal with. For example a 'complaint' about behaviour that has annoyed or concerned you might be harder to make in a call, but it is much more likely to be resolved with your relationship intact by this means than by email. It is a good idea to follow up 'difficult talks' such as these with a positive email of appreciation and summary of what was agreed. In chapter 12 when we look at assertive skills we will introduce a very useful way of preparing what you are going to say (see pages 206–9).

When you do get through, remember to sound positive and warm and always check it is convenient to talk and if so, how long the call is likely to take. We recommend that you stand to make calls whenever possible and do some deep breathing before you pick up the phone. Doing this will ensure that your voice has resonance and energy. Start with a prepared summary of what the call is about and what you would like to achieve. For example: 'I am ringing to explain in a little more detail about how I believe I may be able to help you with … And then I am hoping you will think it worthwhile for us to meet up.'

Enrich your e-connections with appealing snail mail

Most of your correspondence will be done by email but there is still a place for old-fashioned mail in networking. Use it when you want to add some 'feeling tone' to a relationship. We suggest it is also used for most 'greeting-card' and 'thank-you' messages. A handwritten note, especially on elegant quality writing paper or on a beautiful card, will be remembered and appreciated so much more than yet another email or an electronic card. So will cuttings from newspapers or magazines – it shows that you cared enough to find the scissors.

Also snail mail should be used to send hard copies of important reports. (People do not get around to printing out the electronic variety.) This is especially so if you want them to be read by important people. These people often like to read these documents on the plane, train or in bed! You'll notice that laptops are a rare sight in 1st class. Senior people have papers that they whiz through with marker pens. So make life even easier for them and be sure that you have clear headings; abstracts at the start; summaries at the end; and number your paragraphs. They are then more likely to feel positive towards you and pass you on to the relevant connection.

When sending out mail, don't use cheap brown envelopes, second-class stamps or cheap copy paper. It gives an inferior impression. Handwritten envelopes are also more likely to intrigue. (Well they do us anyway!)

11

Proactively build and maintain your relationships

YOU DON'T NEED US TO tell you how important it is to look after your working relationships with colleagues and customers. And, even though this may not be the easiest of tasks for you, it is likely that you already willingly set aside time and possibly a budget for this.

But do you do the same for your networking relationships?

We doubt it. Indeed, we'd be surprised if it ever happens to make your 'To do' list!

Why do we guess this is so? Firstly, because you are human. Don't we all tend to sideline tasks that are not crucial to our current needs? And we know that networking is more about providing for possible future needs than current ones.

Secondly (and perhaps more importantly) our experience leads us to believe that you probably feel more comfortable and are more adept when maintaining relationships where the roles and responsibilities are clearly defined. In networking relationships the roles, boundaries and expectations are essentially informal. There are no established guidelines, best practice, clear protocol or hierarchical structures to guide you. This makes it more difficult for those who worry about getting it right, not putting your foot in it and not upsetting others.

Another problem you could have is that you may approach these relationships in the same way that you do those in your personal life. Because of the way your network connections are often established, they can feel more like social friendships than working relationships. Indeed, to make matters more confusing, they often cross back and forth over the boundary.

You may never have seriously reflected on how your social friendships grew and developed. But it could prove enlightening, in terms of the way you network, if you did. You may discover (along with the majority of our clients) that your social relationships have 'just happened' to you.

Take a quick look right now at your address book of friends and ask yourself how some of these relationships started. Note how many were started by (a) a chance meeting, (b) the other party or (c) enforced circumstances such as having to work or live alongside each other.

We would suggest that most fell into one of these categories. Please note, this is not a criticism! This kind of reactive approach to relationship building may have worked very well in your personal life and some areas of your working life. But in business and career networking this is rarely the case. This is because there are a number of important working assumptions.

The first of these is that the responsibility for creating, maintaining and getting the most out of relationships is equally shared.

A second is that networking for work is fundamentally a 'business' activity and neither a charity nor a pleasure pursuit.

This means that, although a network can sometimes look and behave like one big bunch of friends having fun together, there is an assumption that members are there, first and foremost, for reasons of self-interest. They are primarily there to further their own business or career. Helping you to do the same is also considered part of this process, but making allowances for your confidence problems is rarely part of that bargain. In the democratic, non-hierarchical atmosphere of networking, all members are treated equally whether they have well-developed relationship skills or not. You cannot expect anyone to make a distinction between the nervous novices and the old hands.

You may strike lucky. There are, of course, compassionate people in most networks. Some may spot your problems, and may take it upon themselves to see that you are not left standing in the cold and go out of their way to include you in conversations. If you belong to a networking organisation, some leaders may initiate 'getting to know you' games or help you to use electronic devices that serve the same purpose (such as Ecademy's 50-word profiles – see Wise Owl Know-how, chapter 14, page 235). They may also make an effort to introduce a newcomer to a few potentially useful contacts. But, in our experience, this kind of help has a very limited life. In business networking, once you have been eased 'over the doorstep' towards a new connection, you are then on your own. So with regard to maintenance of the relationships in your network, the ball is always in your court.

However blatantly heartless or unfair these assumptions and facts may seem to those who are sensitive to confidence problems, we believe that they are better worked upon than 'whinged' about. But before you get into action with our tips there is one issue that we would advise you to look at first.

Quality versus quantity

This issue is one that habitually divides the networking world into two camps and continually feeds an impassioned debate – it is the issue of quantity versus quality. You must decide whether you want to focus on getting as many connections as you can or using what energy and time you have to build up a smaller network of relationships with more depth.

You may have already heard the arguments on both sides and know your own mind, but we think it may be useful to briefly summarise the advantages that different people appear to gain from each position. If you want to delve deeper into this issue, read the books and articles written by the people we mention below. (Details of some of their books can be found in Appendix 2, pages 272–3.)

We have observed that the quantity 'bee hive' tends to be particularly attractive to extroverts and people selling products, services or ideas that need to appeal to a mass market. It also attracts people who are actively job hunting and/or testing out new career options. During this period most people need to make more new connections than they would do in normal circumstances.

However, there are many leading networkers who strongly believe that you can only achieve the best results in networking if you concentrate continually in getting as many contacts as you can. Among these are Thomas Power of Ecademy, Carole Stone, London's undisputed 'queen' of the salon and giant networking party world, and Glenda Stone, CEO and founder of Aurora, the fast-growing women's international business network.

Buzzing around the quality 'bee hive', we tend to see many more introverts and people who have complex, high budget or niche products or services to sell. But, again, there are leading figures in the networking world who believe that the best results are obtained from always targeting your energy on a limited number of key contacts. These include the followers of Thomas Dunbar who claimed his research revealed that one person only has the cognitive powers to manage 150 relationships.

A more recent study by David Teten, Donna Fisher and Scott Allen indicated that the best outcomes result from concentrating on the relationships that have a high degree of relevance, trust and credibility. And some currently ongoing research by Rob Cross and Andrew Parker suggests that the most efficient networks are diverse in all respects; offer learning; are drawn from a wide geographical area and contain new and old relationships that are well maintained and add to (rather than drain) your energy levels.

Reading this latest research rang loud bells for us. It reflected many of the problems we have observed in relation to the people who lack confidence. They tend to stay within the comfort zone of the people who are near, whom they have known a long time and with whom they already have good relationships. They also spend an inordinate amount of time sweating about the relationships that haven't much hope of working well and trying tactic after tactic to get non-interested people to like them.

So you can probably guess which bee hive we spend most of our time in!

Yes, we are both fairly firmly rooted in the quality corner. We find that focusing our energy on maintaining relationships with a fairly limited core group of diverse people works for us, but we are both committed to ensuring that we set aside a chunk of time to finding new contacts, especially outside our normal fields of interest.

You need to consider both sides of the debate and then make your own decision in the light of your own current needs. Once you have decided what kind of network you want and how much time you can allocate to building it, try out our tips. They will help you to build and maintain the kinds of relationships you want.

Tips to help you proactively build and maintain your relationships

Get to know them before you meet them

Obviously you won't be able to do this before the start of every relationship, for example, chance meetings. But usually you will know when you are likely to have networking opportunities. Most events now publish a list of attendees. You can study these and select people you might want to meet and look up their profiles on the net or elsewhere. (See Wise Owl Know-how, chapter 14, pages 229–42 for more details.)

Alternatively, you can ask friends and colleagues if they have any information or know anyone in their company or social circle. You can do the same for people you might want to connect to through e-networking. Most electronic-based networks allow profiles to be created by their members.

Pick out information that may help you to understand and empathise with them, as well as subject matter that could be used to start and fuel conversation.

> *'Networking is not just about having a glass of champagne and a chat – you need to know what you want to get out of it and who will be there, get it and get out.'*
>
> Glenda Stone

Make the first move

Most people prefer those who show social initiative. Don't let this 'free' advantage slip away. Copy out this quote from David Schwartz, author of *The Magic of Thinking Big*, and use it to motivate you: 'It is always a big person who walks up to you and offers his/her hand and says hello.'

You could try setting yourself a goal, for example, to make one first move per week for the next month. You will then have replaced a key negative habit with a positive one and be ready for a reward!

Don't dive in, walk into the relationship step by step

Here is a guide to the five steps that build solid foundations for business networking relationships to flourish. Don't skip any!

Step 1: Sniffing out

This is the small talk safety zone (see pages 128–9). Don't be frightened of staying here until your inner butterflies have settled. If the other person wants to go faster, that's tough on them, but it could be even tougher on you and the relationship if you cave in to their agenda.

Step 2: Creating common ground

When you can, start to reveal and probe. But don't forget that your main aim is to develop a professional degree of emotional rapport and empathy rather than find a soul-mate. At first, mention your shared situation in the environment you are both in ('So this is a convenient venue'), and general likes and dislikes rather than business specifics (sports and holidays rather than CVs and annual turnovers). Highlight and nurture any similarities by small acts of kindness (e.g. before the next meeting send the name of that book you recommended and they want to read a.s.a.p.). Finally, move on to finding common business or work interests (such as common experiences with customers or shared frustrations with changes in the law).

If you are meeting face to face, remember your body language and make sure it is reasonably similar to the other person's. The more in tune it is, the quicker rapport will be achieved.

Step 3: Defining differences

This is where you will start to dig and discover the opportunities. It is about clarifying what you've got that he or she hasn't and vice versa. Once you have revealed what you each have to offer and what you each need, be careful not to leap in immediately with a 'sales bid' or request a 'cheeky favour'. Commercial interventions are best put on hold until the next two steps of relationship building have been worked through. In exceptional circumstances, when there is an urgent need, you could, using a casual approach, drop in some information at your next meeting or send it in an email a few days later. If, at the same time, you can give away a 'free' contact or piece of advice, it will help your approach to be perceived as less 'commercial' and more genuinely caring (we are assuming it is!).

Step 4: Testing for trust

If you have decided that there might be some business (or even personal) 'mileage' to be had from developing this relationship, you now need to move the relationship on to a different level. The main object of this step is to test out basic values so that you know whether or not you want to put any trust in each other.

To do this you can begin to tentatively share personal information that might provoke a reaction which could be useful to monitor. For example, this could be revealing: a life dream; a certain work goal; or that you are looking for new openings. On the personal front, someone might share that they have a disability, a problem child or ageing parent. Watching and listening to their reaction will tell you a good deal about the other person's values.

If these kinds of revelations are too difficult, try broaching some slightly trickier subjects than you did in your small talk. Moral dilemmas that you have recently heard aired in the media are good ones to start with as they are already out in the public domain.

After (and only after!) you are happy with their response to your self-disclosures, start tentatively asking more in-depth questions about their business and career background.

Step 5: Maintaining comfortable companionship

This step is about keeping the relationship 'warm' so that it is ready to be used by either party to help you or anyone else in the network to further their business interests. The rest of our tips will show you how to do this.

Commit to maintenance time

Harvey Mackay, author of *Dig Your Well Before You're Thirsty*, suggests that the minimum for keeping up contacts should be at least one hour a week and another for doing your network administration such as sorting information and research. But remember, it won't happen unless you diary it in!

Look for the emotional light beyond the divide

When you meet an apparent mismatch of experience and interests, don't move on immediately. Focus on looking for a match in feelings instead. Look for emotional clues such as changes in tone of voice and eye movements as they talk about their experiences or interests and share having a similar feeling. 'You sound as though that holiday was one you really enjoyed' (it was one you would have hated!). 'It gives me a real lift too when I have had a great holiday. What other holidays have you had that you have enjoyed?' (i.e. not rushing in to tell them about yours which they would probably hate!). Stick to matching positive feelings until you have established a bond with a person with whom you are struggling to empathise. (To become more clued up on body signals, read Peter Collett's *The Book of Tells*, see Recommended books.)

Share weaknesses or mistakes with a smile

This will help you to bond and often opens the other person up because it makes them feel more comfortable with you. If you look miserable while recounting these it will do the opposite. Most people will automatically back off in a networking environment. This is a protective response because they have sensed a mood mismatch. The convention in networking is to maintain an upbeat mood and it does not mean that they might not be very sympathetic in another situation.

Increase your general knowledge of 'trivial' pursuits

This will give you more small talk themes to use, not just at the start of the relationship but to oil its wheels once in motion. Find out more about your network contact's hobbies, pastimes and special interests that have never hitherto taken your fancy. The internet is a great resource for doing this. Pick up information on trends and quirky statistics and use this information as an excuse to make contact and ask their opinion.

Check yourself regularly for prejudice

Yes, you do have them and so do we! Be on the constant look-out for both good and bad ways in which you may be making your perception of people fit in with preconceived ideas you have about their job, role, type of personality or, indeed your first impression of them. We all do this, whether we like to admit it or not. Your prejudice may be right, but it may also be dreadfully wrong. Either way, it will do nothing to enhance the relationship.

Keep a collection of diverse greetings cards and postcards

Keep this handy by your desk. You can dip into this every time you think of telling someone something or giving them a contact and just want to write a quick personal note. Having a diverse collection means that you can quickly choose an appropriate card and this means that it is more likely to get read. It also means that they will notice it more because it will stand out from the rest of the grey-looking mail.

Use their news opportunities

Watch out for news which may be relevant to their area of business or their personal interests. Use these opportunities to make contact. For example, you could write to say that you heard of changes in their company and just hoped that things were going OK for them or send a clipping from a newspaper on developments in a country they hope to work in.

Make contact for contact's sake

Don't wait for ever for the appropriate moment or when you have something particular to say. It is very complimentary to have someone say that they rang or emailed just because they were thinking of you.

Use scrap time as catch-up time

Use waiting in queues to text a good-luck message; the doctor's waiting room to run through your address book and mark the 'Long-time-no-see' contacts; and use train and plane journeys to write catch-up cards.

Become skilful in compliment sharing

Compliment sharing can be an excruciatingly embarrassing affair for people lacking in confidence. This is partly because it tends to be done very clumsily. Make sure you do the following when complimenting:

- **Choose the right moment** – a private one is usually best. Also make sure that this is a time when the other person has the time and emotional energy to absorb what you said.

Don't 'slip' a compliment in as they are rushing out of the door or give one when they are obviously preoccupied.

- **Prepare your body** – breathe deeply and discreetly; look directly at them (not at your shoes!); and then focus on sounding relaxed rather than as terrified as you may feel.
- **Be specific** – praise particular features, behaviours and actions rather than just telling them what a wonderful person they are.
- **Don't put yourself down** – saying you wish you were like them takes away from the compliment because they feel they have to rescue you rather than bask in their own glory.

When receiving a compliment, try to smile and look pleased rather than embarrassed. All you have to do is just say 'Thank you'. Don't get into tit-for-tat behaviour and feel you have to respond with a compliment for them. Show your appreciation at another time – when you have time to prepare yourself.

Be an amateur psychologist, but don't play at it

Get clued up on what makes people tick and use your learning to help you understand your contacts (see Appendix 2, pages 272–3). Don't, however, abuse your knowledge. We all love playing psychometric testing games. We get a great satisfaction from labelling both ourselves and others. Perhaps this is because this gives us an illusion of being more in control and able to influence. But the longer we ourselves are in the 'people business' the more reluctant we have become to do this. It is a very superficial approach to understanding people and unless you are a real expert you can get it very wrong.

So study psychological theories in order to help you empathise and communicate better but don't use them to rigidly 'box up' others in your mind. Otherwise you will start selecting out information about them to fit with the label you have given them and may not notice the changes in them as they develop. Also avoid using psychological terms to describe or chat about people. This will make others prejudge them and doesn't allow for the fact that we can all be different with different people.

Finally, don't give anyone unwanted free analysis!

When building networking relationships (particularly quality ones), it is best to focus on the other person's individuality. Discover, and refer to, the specific traits, experiences, beliefs and aptitudes, which when packaged together make them unique.

Honour cross-cultural codes

For the past 15 years we have had two homes in two very different locations – rural southern Spain and cities in England. We have also travelled widely across the globe and read a good deal about cross-cultural communication. But even now we still sometimes 'put our foot in it' when relating to people in other countries. A common mistake is before meeting up with people, to ask for an appointment and specify a set amount of time. In some cultures, this is actually considered very odd and insulting behaviour unless you are meeting for a specific business transaction. For example, in southern Spain, we are still learning the hard way how to arrange a catch-up meeting with a contact. If you try to arrange a fixed time by saying something like: 'We are coming to Seville this weekend and would like to meet up. Can you make between 6–7 p.m. for tapas at Bar Andalus?'

They might well say 'yes' but there is no guarantee that they will be there! We are much more likely to see them if we say casually, 'We'll be in Seville over the weekend and we'll give you a ring when we get there and see what you are doing.'

Glenda Stone is more expert than we are at this game. Through her network Aurora, she is constantly engaged in cross-cultural networking and she believes it is very important to be aware of the different expectations that people have in different countries. She told us recently:

> *'In the Chinese/Asian culture humbleness is prized. In America visibility and volume are the key. In England, we are concerned about the niceties and protocols involved. In Spain, you have to talk and talk and talk about the family and children before you can talk about business. None of these are better or worse than others – just different.'*

So before networking outside your own familiar territory, find someone who knows the culture or at the very least do some research on the internet or read a book. Then, at least when you do put your foot in it, you can summon up your Unashamed humility (from chapter 6) and apologise!

Have fun together

Don't be worried that this will waste your valuable time. Sharing fun brings people closer. Tune into their sense of humour and have a laugh together.

Pass part of the buck to your family

If you know each other's families, sometimes you may not have to do all the hard maintenance work yourself! If spontaneous bonds between other members of your families develop, it could prove very productive, as this client's story illustrates:

> *Dear Stuart*
>
> *You asked for a little background on how I secured my new post as Director – Business Development and Marketing for a major food business.*
>
> *The role came my way care of Peter X. Peter and I (and our respective wives) were friends in Dubai in 1985 (20 years ago!). His career then took him to Geneva, Nairobi, Birmingham and latterly Kuwait. Mine took me to Cairo, Windsor, Tunis and Beijing. But throughout these years our wives kept in touch and we got together socially whenever we were in the same country.*
>
> *I believe my story demonstrates how important it is to go on nurturing your networking relationships even though they may not appear to offer any obvious business opportunities for many years.*

Recognise and respect 'Get lost' messages

Finally, face reality – you can't win them all! With your strengthened inner confidence you should find this truth a less bitter pill to swallow. But through sheer inexperience you may still find yourself 'flogging dead horses' for too long. Here is a collection of useful 'Get lost' lines from Juliet Erickson's *The Art of Persuasion*:

- Send me a proposal and I'll think about it
- That sounds really interesting; let me get back to you

- We don't have a budget for this
- I've heard this idea before. We've already decided not to do it
- Let's talk again next year
- I'll call you next week when I have …

Give yourself full permission to back off when you hear these. Or, indeed, when you see the obvious non-verbal clues such as clock-watching or wandering eyes or a yawn! And, don't forget that you can use the polite signals yourself as well!

12

Assertively protect yourself and others

HERE COMES THE STING FOR your tail – the assertiveness skills!

Let's hope that you never need their protection. If you have been putting our tips into action so far, your Cool Cat Qualities and at least half of your Buzzy Bee Skills should be working their magic. Your increased glow of confidence should be warning off most hostile 'predators'. But there are always exceptions. There are people who may act in an insensitive manner perhaps because they are too preoccupied, too stressed or too arrogant to pick up the hint from subtle indicators.

How self-protective or protective of others are you when you encounter a 'predator'? Here's a little test. Consider how you might react and respond when faced with a networker who was behaving in the following kinds of ways. Would you feel upset and/or angry? Would you ignore the behaviour or would you confront the person? Would you be proud of the way you responded?

- Being mischievous and poking fun at you or others even when it is highly inappropriate or ill-mannered to do so, e.g. 'Do I detect a trace of east London in your accent – so you must be called ...!'
- Continually asking for more 'cheeky' favours and never giving in return, e.g. 'Would you photocopy the attendee list for me? I'm so busy nowadays that I don't get to meetings.'
- Being schmoozy spongers, e.g. 'They obviously like your face behind that bar, you always get served. If you get these, I'll get the drinks next week.' ... but next week never comes!
- Using you as a handy (and safe) punch-bag, e.g. they have had a row with the boss and then snap your head off when you innocently comment on the temperature of the room.
- Getting a kick out of making others feel small beside them, e.g. 'Oh you're in that department. I used to deal with your manager when I was head of purchasing.'
- Being snide because they resent people who are winners or likely to win, e.g. 'Can I introduce you to Sophie? She was obviously born with a shinier silver spoon than us – she's already a partner in her firm at the tender age of 32.'
- Expressing continual cynicism or sabotaging others' progress, e.g. withholding important connections or information about opportunities without good reason.
- Being plain ruthless and appearing not to care who or what gets hurt in their effort to achieve what they want, e.g. will lie and cheat to get a connection or sale.

If you don't think you would cope that well with this kind of 'predatory' behaviour, you are in good company. We work with people in every echelon of society who are also too intimidated to be assertive. You may never see them shrinking or quaking, because they have acquired tricks to cover up these feelings. For example, they might make an excuse to walk away from a difficult conversation with these 'predators'. Or, they pretend they are too busy to take a call or reply to the email from them. Alternatively, they cover up their fear of them with outright aggression and may bully them from their positions of power. For example, they may have a word in the ear of someone who could refuse their business or they give them a very public put-down in front of an important connection.

You may think that anyone who behaves in such a way deserves this kind of treatment and that should be the end of the story. But, we know it rarely is. If you respond in such a passive or aggressive way your self-esteem and confidence take a dive. Furthermore, the issue has not been dealt with. The 'predator' still retains the power to make you feel small or 'trick' you into behaving in a way that will diminish your self-respect.

But that's not all. You may lose out because most 'predators' in networking are really not predators at all. They are just behaving badly out of habit or because they 'know no better'. For one reason or other, they haven't fully appreciated the democratic, reciprocal and ethical nature of the networking world. Penny Power, a founder and director of Ecademy, confirmed this. She recently told us: 'I get about ten alerts to unreasonable behaviour every week. The vast majority are just advising me that a member is selling rather than networking These people are putting themselves and the transaction before the relationship. They only need to be taught and they always respond gratefully.'

But how do you 'teach them'? That's the question no doubt you now want us to answer fast!

We believe that by far the most successful way is to give the person who is out-of-line a slight 'sting' with an assertive approach. By this we mean one that is:

- direct – criticism is given directly to the person concerned rather than complaining about them to others
- ethically driven – derived from a common code of ethics but is non-lecturing in its delivery style
- win/win – focused whenever possible on the benefits of a resolution for both parties
- respectful – well mannered even if the person is downright rude
- rational – uses rational argument and facts rather than emotional 'pulls' and 'pushes' or knee-jerked feelings to make the point
- reasonable – makes realistic, achievable requests
- calm – like a Cool Cat!

This kind of approach will usually stop the 'bad' behaviour and elicit an apology. But additionally, the person is sometimes so remorseful that they fall over themselves to make it up to you with not-to-be-sniffed-at favours.

Don't believe us? Try our tips before giving in or giving up.

Tips to help you assertively protect yourself and others

Learn so you can lean on codes of conduct

Don't attempt to assert yourself unless you are convinced of your moral right to do so. We have already looked at the important issue of moral codes in Cool Cat Qualities, chapter 3 Incorruptible integrity, so if the organisation in which you are networking doesn't have an obvious code, you already have some clear inner principles to guide you.

If you are networking internationally, take special care to check out the codes of social conduct that are specific to the country you are connecting in. Certainly what is considered aggressive behaviour varies considerably from continent to continent. (See page 196 for more on this.)

Disagree agreeably

'Predators' love to start an argument and are often aggressively provocative just for the hell of it. But don't rise to the bait even if you are sorely tempted to do so. Stay cool. Networking environments are rarely good places to have a heated argument. This is because they threaten the positive and social atmosphere that is needed. Instead, make a response like those shown in one of our examples below. You'll notice that these agree in part or suggest that you could (but you don't have to!) agree. But they also give a clear and polite message that you have no intention of pursuing the argument.

'That's certainly worth debating, but I'd rather not go down that avenue just now. . . . How much longer is it until the speaker starts? I am looking forward to this talk.'

'You may well have a point, but we'd need more time than we have on this plane journey to get to grips with that issue. You said you've been in Berlin several times before . . . was that on business?'

Deal later with put-downs

In the 'nice' social atmosphere of networking put-downs are most likely to come with a sugar coating. You may not even notice that you are receiving them. So don't worry if you can't deal assertively with them at the time they are given. In our next tip, we are going to introduce you to a strategy you can use to politely confront the put-downer and ask them to stop this behaviour. But the first step is to become more skilled at spotting when you have been given one. Here are some examples of common put-downs that are usually delivered with great charm.

- Lecturing down – knowing better than you do what is good for you e.g. 'Isn't that running before you can walk? I would have thought you'd be best starting with …'
- Insulting labels – putting someone into a 'box' with many others that has negative connotations e.g. 'You women always …'
- Ignoring or topping success stories e.g.

Derek: *'John, do you remember Anna, from Birmingham? She's just won a very prestigious book award.'*

John: *'Yes, I remember the charming Brummy twang! I don't think I told you that we have an office there but I avoid going there whenever I can. It's not the most attractive city is it?*

Anna: *'No I suppose it isn't. Where is your office exactly?'*

- Watch out for this kind of behaviour. Stay cool and make a vow to deal with it later when you have time to prepare a well-crafted assertive request for a change in their behaviour.

Script requests for a change of behaviour

This is our favourite assertiveness strategy. We have been teaching it for over 30 years and are still in awe of its power. It can be used in innumerable situations outside the arena of networking as well, so it is well worth perfecting it. (It has helped get many a noisy neighbour to turn down the volume or even got lots of argumentative children to bed on time!)

We suggest that you use the following 'template' to compose and rehearse your request before talking to the person who has put you down or is using any of the other kind of 'predator' behaviours that we discussed earlier in this chapter.

Ideally, your script is best composed with the help of another person. This is because this kind of 'threatening' behaviour has a strong emotional impact on us (even though we may hate to admit it). Our subconscious primitive instinct to 'fight' back or 'take flight' will inevitably have been activated. As a result we may use aggressive or passive language without even realising we are doing so. When another person is helping you they are more likely to notice whether you have, for example, unconsciously slipped in a counterproductive snide remark or self-effacing remark.

Once you have written your script (using confident language, pages 156–9), practise saying it out loud. Make sure that it is accompanied by confident body language (see pages 160–1). Rehearse it until you feel relaxed and it sounds natural. You can add a few 'filler' words to make it run more smoothly, but don't change the order of the sections and don't be tempted to leave any out. It has been constructed in such a way that it will keep the attention of the other person. It will make them feel understood and 'hook' them into wanting to change their behaviour. Believe us, it works like a dream.

Assertive Scripting: template for composing a polite and persuasive request for a change of behaviour

Section 1: Explanation

Summarise in one or two sentences the problem or situation. Use objective language, facts, dates and statistics rather than feelings or impressions.

Examples (examples (a), (b) and (c) follow on through the template):

(a) Each time you have introduced me to someone recently, you have called me one of those city lawyers who milk us all dry. (i.e. for a labelling put-down)

(b) When we met last month, you told me that I was too old to be considered for most new management posts. (i.e. for an insensitive and discouraging judgement)

(c) The last two times we met you also asked if I'd mind getting the drinks and that you would pay me next time. (i.e. for confronting scroungers)

Section 2: Feelings

Make an appropriate statement acknowledging your own

feelings (remember that in a business networking environment this would be 'I'm concerned' rather than 'I'm frightened').

Empathise (without patronising) with the other persons' feelings or situation.

Examples:

(a) I was irritated by this. I know you were only joking, so you might think I am being oversensitive but ...

(b) I felt embarrassed being reminded in this environment of my age. I appreciate that you may have only being trying to help me with your experience but ...

(c) I haven't been too worried about this as I appreciate you may have forgotten, so ...

Section 3: Needs

Request the specific change of behaviour you want. Offer to compromise or negotiate if this is appropriate to the situation.

Examples:

(a) ... I'd prefer you to just introduce me by my name

(b) ... I'd rather you didn't bring up my age again

(c) ... I'm happy to wipe the slate clean but suggest we get our own drinks in future

Section 4: Consequences

Compose a sentence that finishes your scripted request on a positive note. When it is appropriate, outline any pay-off the other person can expect for complying with your request. In networking, the pay-off could be implicitly rather than explicitly expressed. For example, the pay-off is usually that you will continue to value and respect them as a networking contact.

Examples:

(a) I'd feel a lot happier if I could explain my role in my own way. I hope you understand

(b) I hope you don't mind me mentioning this because I do enjoy and value your company

(c) That way we'll avoid any confusion over whose turn it is to pay

Ask critics for clarification

As we know, confident networking takes us out of our comfort zone in relation to the people with whom we spend time. In the course of extending our horizons, we potentially expose ourselves to increased criticism from people who don't share our values and opinions. There may be some who also consider us rivals and may use criticism as a competitive tool in the game of one-upmanship.

Don't be alarmed by this news – just be ready for it. First, gear yourself up to respond positively – yes, positively! Criticism can be very useful information. What has been said could be an invaluable eye-opener to a weakness in your personality, belief system or working practice. Or it could be a useful revelation about how you can be perceived by others.

So a confident person doesn't immediately leap in to defend themselves. First, you often hear them say something like: 'That's an interesting point of view. That's not been my experience. What makes you think that?'

By asking for clarification, you can distinguish constructive critics from the destructive ones. If the critic responds with interesting or new information you can simply learn from it, or use it to fuel a continuing debate.

If, on the other hand, the critic cannot clarify the argument, and gives a destructive response such as 'No – but it sounds like a naïve point of view to me', you can then use another technique to block them from continuing. The most effective way to do this is with a classic assertiveness strategy called 'Fogging'. This simply involves responding back in a way that appears to indicate that you are agreeing. For example:

'You could be right.'

'You may have a point there.'

'It is possible, I suppose, to look at it that way.'

This technique can also be very useful if you want to stop an argument in its tracks for other reasons as well. Perhaps you want to stay at Level 1 in the conversation and stick to safe small talk (remember pages 128–9). Or, perhaps you want to exit the conversation to move on and meet someone else.

A word of warning – when networking, never overuse this technique. It will certainly protect you, but is not the best way to gain friends and build great connections!

Starve the gossips

First, we should come clean – we love a good gossip. In the confidential confines of a good friendship, it is fun and a great release for those negative feelings we should be ashamed of! But in the world of networking it must be avoided. It is not good for you or your reputation and it could seriously harm someone else. The networking environment can be a fertile breeding ground for Chinese whispers. A harmless gossipy remark can be passed on and on and, in the process, become an unrecognisable and ugly untruth.

So, if you hear any gossip (and you will!), just give a 'cut-off' response such as:

'Oh really, I don't tend to listen to rumours . . . The food here is getting better I think, don't you?'

'Wouldn't know about that – and I am actually not that interested either – I find him a very generous connector. He is always putting people in touch with each other.'

'Sounds a bit too much like gossip to me – I don't get into that.'

Face festering feelings

In the social atmosphere of networking, we grin and bear most of our minor irritations and grumbles. But if somebody, or something, has been bugging you for a while and you feel your negative feelings escalating, deal assertively with them fast. If you do not, these feelings could escalate into anger or turn inwards and become depression or cynicism. Ideally, before you take action, talk through your feelings and the problem with a good friend. Choose one who you can count on to take a sensible rather than empathic view ('Oh, I know. Isn't she awful!' won't help). Business networking, as we have said before, is not an environment where you should expect to have your emotional wounds healed.

Your focus must be on finding a workable solution to the problem. First, try the Assertive Scripting technique we discussed on pages 206–9 to make a reasonable request. If this doesn't work, you may need to get a super-assertive co-networker to help you negotiate a compromise solution. Finally, if neither one of these approaches work, try scripting an assertive request to the 'management' if one exists. If it doesn't, or cannot help, abandon this contact and move on. The world is full of other sources of networking nectar – there is no need to stay in a nest of wasps and be stung for the rest of your working life.

13

Build a distinctive reputation

OSCAR WILDE IS REPUTED TO have said: 'One can survive everything nowadays, except death, and live down anything except a good reputation.'

If only good reputations were so solid! With the kind of mass media we have these days, they can be transformed into disastrous ones overnight. Unfortunately, one 'law' of today's mass media is that bad news about people is guaranteed to travel faster and more widely than good news. A second is that, the more successful someone has been, the more interest will be taken and the third is that if the 'facts' that caused that reputation to suffer are found to have been misrepresented, very little mileage can be made of this good news.

No one can now afford to sit on their laurels or take their halos for granted. A good reputation is much too vulnerable. It has to be constantly nurtured and well maintained. This is especially so in the world of networking because your reputation is your currency. It is what 'buys' you trust and 'buys' you connections. This is why, as we discussed in chapter 3, Cool Cats always ensure that they have 'Incorruptible integrity'.

But even a reputation built on impeccable qualifications and integrity of pure gold is useless unless it is visible. We found this following true story inspiring and hope you do too.

CASE STUDY

Richard, a client of Stuart's, was concerned that his role as an industry watch-dog might end in the not-too-distant future. He didn't want to leave his job prematurely, but he felt that he ought to do something to ensure that he would be more employable should he be made redundant. He therefore set about enhancing his reputation within the industry. He made himself available to talks, business briefings and presented at conferences. He wrote articles and went out of his way to be present at as many meetings as possible so that he had more face-to-face contacts with people in his network. He became known for being not only a distinguished expert but a great source of contacts. When a year later, a rumour began to circulate that what he feared might happen was on the cards, he was contacted and offered a number of ideal posts. By the time he was made redundant he had a tempting pile from which to make his choice.

Your reputation is not just vital for your work today; it is also the best insurance you can provide for your career. None of us can be sure that we will still have the same job, business or profession throughout our working life. And, increasingly, that is not what most people want anyway. The expert in career transition Herminia Ibarra stresses that: 'Nowadays, your reputation beyond your immediate circle and current employer is more important than ever before.'

Networking is a very powerful means of ensuring that a very wide range of people know, in short:

- you exist
- what you stand for
- the kind of results you can achieve
- that you are highly approachable and collaborative, and, of course,
- that you have super confidence!

So don't hide your light under the proverbial bushel. Make sure you shine brightly and distinctively and can be seen by anyone and everyone.

Tips for building a distinctive reputation

Brand yourself with panache

There is a vogue for what has become known as 'personal branding', which is a distinctive way of marketing you and what you stand for. This trend may reflect the growing numbers of people who are self-employed, but this subject is also attracting the attention of many others as well. Examples are people going through a career transition and those who may be considering one and want to keep that option open. It is very much easier to make career and job changes if you have a distinguishing personal brand than if you are known merely as the representative of someone else's brand. For example, if people were talking about you without mentioning the company you worked for, there would be certain distinguishing features that most people who knew you would instantly remember and possibly use to describe you to others.

To clarify what we mean, here are some sets of features of two people who have a strong personal brand. Most people who know them would, at the mention of their name, probably instantly recall these individual features that they have ensured are built into their reputation. This has been done through their adoption of a consistent style of behaviour, self-presentation, sharing and way of relating to others.

Bill is the man who:

- is internationally credited with successfully setting up mobile telephone networks in the most remote corners of the world
- is passionate about making phone masts blend with the countryside
- believes that big business can be socially responsible as well as commercially successfully
- is always meticulously dressed in designer suits with bright ties
- has a schoolboy sense of humour and fun
- comes up with practical solutions for all kinds of 'impossible' challenges
- is a triathlon champion,

and is not just known as 'a senior manager from Vodafone'! (So if you were headhunting for someone to head up a new ecological project in Africa you might seek out Bill himself or ask him for a contact.)

Karen is the woman who:

- led a major research project in HRT
- is passionate about women's rights to make their own health decisions
- is a living role model of how to have a successful career and bring up four happy children
- believes in the positive power of the media and is constantly using it to campaign for causes
- wears distinctive jewellery that is handmade by her artist daughter
- has a wealth of contacts in high places and is always willing to share them appropriately
- is a great listener and mentor of young professionals,

and is not just known as 'a nurse manager from BUPA'! (So if you were a TV producer and you wanted to make a programme aimed at young working mothers you would almost certainly be given Karen's name as a contact.)

As someone whose inclination may be to stay in the shadows rather than the limelight, personal branding won't come naturally to you. But remember, the concept behind it is very simple. You just regard yourself as a product that needs to be sold – not just once, but repeatedly to a following of loyal customers who refuse to settle for anything less than the best – i.e. You!

Once you have adopted that mind-set the rest is pretty easy. It is not rocket science and you don't need to spend a fortune to make it happen. You are already more than halfway there anyway. You have done a considerable amount of the basic work when thinking earlier about making an instant impact with your image (see Buzzy Bee Skills, chapter 8).

You could pick up some hints from the example of the commercial giants:

- Think big and wide – don't sweat the details.
- Select a specialism – centre all your publicity and self-presentation materials around a core message, which highlights preferably just one, or at most three strengths and/or complementary skills or services. Don't be a chameleon and attempt to sell yourself as a Jack or Jill of all Trades.
- Match your market – keep your image in tune with your target market. For example, if they are designer junkies, clothes, accessories, car and website must be the latest fad; if they are the bargain hunter variety – keep to the plain and functional.
- Use a simple strapline – over and over again (remember your elevator pitch from pages 114–20).
- Choose one or two dominant colours when working and stick with them. (Like EasyJet and Virgin!) Ensure these are reflected as often as possible in your stationery, accessories and publicity, photos and products, web presence and also your clothes. Or, choose another distinguishing aspect of your 'look' to make your special feature such as a 'smart' or 'funky' dress style, special ties or interesting hats.
- Distinguish yourself from competitors – highlight the differences but without demeaning them (i.e. don't do what politicians are wont to do!).

Be a third-party networking node

This is one of the very best ways to build a solid reputation within a network. Become a person who is always introducing people to each other. But don't just wait to be asked or for chance to offer you an opportunity (e.g. two people happening to be at the same conference or party). Make it happen routinely. Each time you are reviewing or entering a new person into your contact list, set aside a few minutes to think whether or not it might be worth putting any of your contacts in touch with each other. Remember, it is not your job to know how they might work together; you just need to have a 'hunch' that they would benefit from making contact happen or that they might enjoy each other's company.

Once you have made the introduction, don't forget to check up whether or not it has been useful. This is the way you will learn how to become a more effective node, but it will also demonstrate that you care and will build your reputation as a serious and committed networker.

Become a gentle mood enhancer

Smiles are more addictively attractive than frowns. In the long term, people will veer towards those who make them feel good. A moaner might attract attention while they need to nurse a wound or air a grievance. But it won't last. Primitive instinct sends most people in search of the positive survivors. So when you are out and about, smile regularly even when you don't much feel like it.

Another obvious way to enhance another's mood is to compliment them. Be generous with compliments and remember how to give them well (see pages 194–5).

There are many other ways to enhance moods, such as focusing on positive possibilities, recounting good news, funny stories and being nurturing. A well-timed offer of a cup of tea can be just as uplifting as vintage champagne.

But don't overdo it! Persistently happy-clappy people are a put-off too. In the long term people are attracted to those who exude calmness as well as positive energy. Aren't these the kinds of people you would turn to for help, advice or a dependable service when you needed it? That's the kind of reputation you want in networking.

Be an indispensable dogsbody

In the running of every organisation (work and social) there are always small tasks that are in no one's job description and, because they lack obvious kudos, very few people want to do them. They are ideal opportunities for people who lack confidence. They are a low-risk way to gain instant popularity and make your name known. This could include, for example, being the person that offers to get the cakes for meetings or chases people for donations for a charity event.

Obviously, playing dogsbody is not a role that you would want full time or for ever, but it is a good way of making a positive impact without much effort and should be given serious consideration. If you do it well and are obviously earning brownie points by the dozen as a result, you won't be in the role for long. Trust that the queue to replace you will start to form.

Make life easier for the journalists

If you think your world is fast paced and competitive, try being a journalist. They are in an over-populated and low-paid profession with nil job security. Between us, we have met many hundreds in both the business and mass media, and would be hard-pressed to name even a handful who could be described as cool, calm and collected. (No offence to journalists – just empathy!) This is why our best overall tip for building a good reputation with them is to make their life a little easier. You have to get to know each journalist well to know how to do this best, but here are some secrets based on personal experience:

- Send short, punchy press releases – with the bulleted sound-bites and statistics that are easy to copy and paste straight into an article.
- Be proactive – send them stories and tit-bits of information, especially those which relate to big-news stories.
- Make your message newsworthy – that will please their editor because it is news that sells.
- Don't put them in your regular newsgroup list – select out very short relevant extracts from newsletters and reports and email with web links that will take them to further info if they need it.
- Use the language that they would use – this means reading the journals they write for and knowing their core market.
- Specify availability – give times when they could ring for an interview – one could be diaried immediately.
- Ask for pre-interview information – the best professionals are now in the habit of doing this. They know it saves their time as well as yours. You can then prepare short, snappy answers to their questions.
- Ask them how they are doing and how their lives are going – try to pick up information about their lives so you can

build a relationship by more meaningful small chat. Also try to relate your information to issues you know may be of personal interest to them. (Journalists are human and will write better articles on subjects that get to their heart.)

- Be upbeat – if you are giving bad news, give possible solutions as well. (The latter may not get printed, but at least you will have lifted the spirits of the journalist who overdoses on bad news every day.)
- Don't complain when they misquote you – unless they have seriously damaged your reputation. It's trite but true – 'Bad publicity is better than no publicity.' The words will be constantly misinterpreted and altered to fit with the theme of the article or story of the day. That is the 'game' and journalists don't come back to people who can't 'take the heat'. So have a moan to your friends and give yourself a treat rather than rushing towards the arms of a lawyer.

Finally, if you want to use the media to help you build a reputation, remember you need them more than they need you! This point is reinforced by Simon Barker, director of PR company Cubitt Consulting Ltd, who offered us these tips.

> *'There are two key things you can do. Firstly, most of the specialist industry media publish a list of scheduled features for the year. Call up the features editors and ask them to email you the lists. Look through to see if any articles are relevant to your expertise. Then re-contact the features editor at least one month prior to the publishing date and ask for the contact details of the commissioned journalist. Contact them and offer your point of view. They may wish to receive it in writing, rather than have a discussion over the*

phone. Ensure that what you have to say is succinct and incorporates opinion, figures and examples.

Secondly, if you have a strong opinion or supplementary information to a piece of industry news that is in the media and is likely to be ongoing, telephone the reporters who have covered the story and offer your opinion.'

Get writing or find a ghost

After reading our last tip, you may have decided that you prefer to be the one that writes. Not a bad idea if you can do it. At least give it a try. But be warned, if you are successful at it, the journalists will soon be swarming around you so you will have to deal with them!

Being the author of numerous articles, leaflets, reports or newsletters will certainly add credibility to your reputation. But of course the writing has to be readable. The more mass-readable it is the better. This is very much harder and more time-consuming to do than most people think. So it may well be worthwhile to employ a 'ghost-writer'. You'd be surprised to learn how many are out there. Most journalists and many people working in publishing now write in the name of others on a very regular basis. There are also many freelance writers who specialise in writing reports for people in business. So don't feel shy about turning to professionals for this kind of help – if the celebrities and executives have their secret ghosts, so can you.

Give talks to whoever and wherever

Don't be too proud to give a talk to whoever will listen to you. Gael has had years of experience of giving talks in dingy venues to audiences of two or three, and has no regrets. Firstly, it built her confidence and expertise. She was able to make her worst learning gaffes in front of audiences who were naturally sympathetic. (If you are an audience of two, you are especially grateful to any speaker who thinks you are still special enough to talk to.)

Secondly, she found that in the intimate atmosphere of these kinds of occasions, people tend to give honest feedback and invaluable ideas more freely.

Thirdly, she has found unexpected golden geese amongst the tiniest of crowds. There is always the possibility that one person is only that famous six degrees of separation away from another who could catapult your career forward.

Start by offering yourself to small clubs or chambers of commerce. They are always looking for speakers. Try to stick to your specialist subject, but also listen to what they may be asking for and what specific needs they have. It is always good to wrap your standard 'talk' in packaging that is appealing and relevant to each audience. You will quickly lose your reputation on the circuit if you don't do that.

Take care to check that the profile that you send the organiser of a talk is updated and will have relevant appeal. Don't be shy about your successes because this profile is going to be read by not just the people in that organisation, but possibly by many thousands of others, as most talks and speaker details are published in the internet. It is a good idea to include a link to your website or web profile as well for this reason.

'Toastmasters' (see chapter 18, page 260) has a good reputation for helping develop public speaking skills and confidence. They also have many contacts and will advise you on how to get speaking engagements.

Become a party animal – throw a party, attend relevant social gatherings

Go on, force yourself! Parties may not be your scene. But to build a reputation you must be visible. Go to be seen, not to enjoy yourself. Adopting a means-to-an-end mind-set will help. Give yourself full permission to 'drop in' only for an hour. But while you are there, look as though you are having fun, share your success and make yourself popular by offering to fill glasses and plates. (This is a great way to be noticed and gives you an easy way of circulating and starting up conversations.)

No invitations? Then throw parties yourself. This will make you even more popular and enhance your reputation. Carole Stone, the queen of networking parties in England, was once, in her own words, 'painfully shy' and now has over 42,000 names in her contact list. (For details of her book on the subject, see Appendix 2; pages 272–3.)

If you don't want to go that far out of your comfort zone, why not offer to help others organise their parties? Perhaps you could do the wine or co-ordinate the food or deal with the guest list. Very few people would refuse such an offer. This way you will keep a background role, but still be in a great position to meet other people and make your name known for very little effort (or expense!).

Start a club – ensure interest in theme/purpose, engage supporters

Another relatively easy way to build your reputation is to start a club. In the process of promoting the club your name will be noticed by hundreds of people even if only five people actually attend the meetings. Gael was recently invited to give a talk at one of Ecademy's most successful local clubs. She was interested to hear its organiser, Larry Osei-Kwaku, had never done anything like this before and did it specifically as a confidence building strategy for himself. Gael subsequently wrote to him to find out whether his plan had worked and received this heart-warming email in reply:

CASE STUDY

Hello Gael

Good to hear from you.

I think starting the networking club has boosted not just my confidence but others' too. One of the regular attendees says he comes because he claims it boosts his self-esteem. I didn't even know I was that open and warm a person until I started running the club.

An alternative to starting a work-focused club could be to start a social one in your community. This would enhance your reputation locally with people who might not even know you existed otherwise. We have started a couple of book clubs and an Argentine tango club in different towns where we have lived. None of these projects were demanding or costly to organise and through them we have had great fun as well as meeting many new interesting work contacts.

And, of course, if you find you take to the limelight, in these days of global communication networks, it is not that difficult for the national and world club scenes to become your reputation-building oysters!

PART THREE

•

Wise Owl Know-how

In this section, you will learn how to acquire the wisdom that super-confident networkers have and can depend on. Their up-to-date and relevant knowledge in six specific areas that are key to becoming a super-confident networker gives added support and impetus to their inner and outer confidence. Like Wise Owls they are fast and efficient fliers. They use their perceptive vision to seek out crucial information, and they use their acute hearing to pick up news of the latest resources and research. They watch, wait and plan before setting out to hunt. Their nests and heads are so full to the brim with wisdom that they are confident that their perch at the top of the networking tree is secure and unassailable. No wonder there is always a flock of fledglings jostling for a chance to meet them and pick their brains.

14

Know where to connect

Make the best of your usual face-to-face scenarios

MOST NETWORK CONNECTIONS ARE STILL being made in the traditional way through relationships with colleagues and also work and associated organisations that you may already know about. But do you know them all, belong to enough of them and attend their meetings regularly? And, do you use them well enough for networking purposes? How many new connections, for example, have you made in these during the last year? How well do you nurture relationships with the people you consider to be key contacts?

In your work setting, aim particularly to connect well with those involved in 'big picture' issues such as strategy and human resources. If your company is part of a group with various affiliates, subsidiaries, divisions etc., check out the key individuals in those areas too. Try to find ways of socialising with them. They probably attend meetings or conferences that you could go to. Seek them out in coffee breaks and introduce yourself and engage in some small talk – but remember these are not the places to do a heavy sell about you, your ideas or your services and products!

Having meals with colleagues and clients is just one informal way you can build a relationship. This is an extract from an email we had from a client that illustrates the advantages of networking in this way:

> *'The power of the networking over dinner had done what many applications and interviews had failed to do. Networking had allowed me to express me, as me, in a way that was relevant to the client and without veneer.'*

Joining professional associations is another usual scenario for networking. Most now have their own websites. They not only provide details of their key people, they also give speaker biographies and contact details. Increasingly, many also provide 'attendee' or 'delegate' listings for their events. Sometimes you have to register your own details first before you are allowed to see such a list, but we recommend this as a great way of finding old and new contacts.

If you are employed, check which associations your company belongs to and ask to represent your company at association events, or at least attend with the nominated representative. There are over 32,000 professional associations in the UK, and it is inevitable that there will be at least one of relevance to you. It's simply a case of searching on the internet or, even better, enquiring through a trusted acquaintance! A sample listing of a small number of these appears on pages 268–71 in Appendix 1.

And remember, these are not just good places to meet like-minded people from other organisations in your field, they are often good for meeting recruiters too as this story from a client illustrates:

> *'Maria became a member of the Women In Technology International network. She was a full-time employee of a large IT corporation but was made redundant. Her company provided her with outplacement support; however, she was unsuccessful in finding a new employer. She continued to attend bi-monthly WITI meetings, and happened to talk to me there about her lack of success in finding a new role. I enquired as to her background and skills. It turned out that she was a perfect fit for a contract role I was trying to recruit a suitable candidate for, within another large IT corporation.'*
>
> Carole, *business development director in IT*

Increase your unusual face-to-face opportunities

There are scenarios in your social and personal life which can also be great resources of connections for work as well as friendship. Some people make it a rule to keep their personal lives completely separate from their working lives. We believe that a hard and fast rule is not necessary when you have enough confidence to say 'no' whenever you want to do so. There are many advantages to be had from keeping some flexible boundaries.

An alternative is to designate one or two areas as strictly 'private'. Then try to extend your social network into undiscovered areas where you might have looser boundaries and find some potentially interesting new work connections. As Harvey

Mackay says in *Dig Your Well Before You're Thirsty*, 'if everyone in your network is the same as you, it isn't a network, it's an anthill.' Bringing connections in from your social life to your working life is often very stimulating and eye-opening. This is especially true if you are looking for ways to expand or change the direction of your career, as Herminia Ibarra, one of the world's great experts in this field, points out:

> *'The acquaintances, neighbours and co-workers who operate in the same spheres as we do can rarely tell us something we don't already know because they hear about the same things we do. . . . the only way to make a true career change is by shifting connections from the core to the periphery of our networks. It is often strangers who help us make sense of where we are going and who we will become.'*

Or, if you want to build some career 'insurance', another well-known networking guru and author of *It's Not Business, It's Personal*, Ronna Lichtenberg suggests:

> *'Limiting yourself to relationships with people who are like you, who see the world in the same way you do, is one of the most dangerous things you can do in your career. It's smooth and wonderful, it feels great, it's congenial, it's collegial, it's reassuring. It's all of those things until the day you walk off the edge of a cliff that no one in your crowd even noticed was there.'*

So ask yourself does your social network extend as far as it could? And when you are socialising, are you keeping your ears and eyes open for connections that could be mutually beneficial for you or others in the work sphere? Here are some examples of the kinds of organisations that have helped many people we know find interesting new contacts:

- Alumni organisations – many school, university and professional postgraduate courses promote alumni groups to foster the reputation of their own institutions. These can prove very beneficial breeding grounds for maintaining and creating networking connections. Most have websites with member listings and discussion areas.
- Sports and health clubs – don't be too keen to rush through your workouts – a little hanging about in changing rooms has produced many a good business deal.
- Parent associations – examples of these would be traditional Parent Teacher Associations and smaller groups such as Working Mother clubs. Children's education and the stresses of parenting provide a strong common bond and make it much easier to start friendships.
- Special interest groups, clubs and classes – the leaders of church groups, language, dance and cookery classes, pressure and political groups all know that one of the main reasons people join them is to meet others. So don't be left out because you don't consider yourself interested enough in the subject matter!
- Local community involvement – this is one of the best ways to make work and career connections through your personal life. Residents associations and community action groups attract movers and shakers.
- Voluntary/charitable activities – giving of your time to these kinds of activities will strengthen your self-esteem and so is good for your inner confidence. But many people also make

great connections through their charitable work. By being involved with these, you are openly displaying the values that will make you instantly likeable and attractive in terms of trust to others in the networking world. Remember also that it is common for high-level people from the world of work to commit time and energy to charities and, while in this territory, you may find such people less daunting. These kinds of individuals are also often on the look-out for good quality people, and will pass on contacts even if they don't need them themselves as this story illustrates:

> *'Bob had his own small IT business. However, with the IT market downturn a few years ago, he was finding that his company was experiencing limited success. He was mentioned to me by a contact I know through my voluntary work. I met him at a charity fundraising event, and suggested that he send me his CV. His skills just happened to fit with a requirement that my company had at that time for a contractor. Bob has now been with the company for over three years. He has also introduced another past colleague of his who has been engaged on a contract basis.'*

- Hairdressers and nail bars – these kinds of venues have been mentioned on Stuart's networking courses as being examples of where good business contacts can be made.

Online social and business networks

There are approximately 60 so-called online social networking platforms that have developed a substantial following. However, the vast majority are quite disappointing in their lack of diversity, business or career focus, and low levels of functionality, including privacy options.

Two of the more successful online networks are the US-based www.ryze.com and the UK-based www.ecademy.com Both of them have lots of flexible options about privacy, and use very rich functionality to help you search and connect quickly with relevant others, as well as offering vibrant discussion forums and a wide range of active clubs.

Ecademy, for example, allows you to tap into a well-developed online community of mainly, but not exclusively, small business entrepreneurs. Its key features include:

- Profile page – for posting information about you that is likely to be of interest and appeal to this community. Adding a small photo of you makes you 'more real' and apparently increases your 'page hit' rate by over 50 per cent. You can also add logos and hyperlinks, so that this page can give the appearance of being almost like your personal website. Additionally, you have the option of inserting '50 Words' about you, which then allows you to 'Find Other People Like You' within this currently 55,000-member online community.

- Profile hits – you can see who's been peeking at your profile – and then contact them.

- Clubs – over 1,100 ready-made clubs including topic-based clubs such as 'The Outsourcing Club', 'The Human Resources Club', as well as geographically based clubs such as the 'Guildford Ecademy Club' for local meetings. You can even create your own club – just as Gael did. She created 'The Confidence Club' (www.confidenceclinic.com).

- Regular 'live' events. The site features very helpful event functionality, making it very simple to organise an event, and allowing attendees, or those considering attending, to see the profiles of those already registered, with whom they can make contact in advance.

- Discussion areas are available for posting weblogs and commenting on others' weblogs – a great way of raising awareness and getting known for your specialism. Due to the high visibility of this platform, it means your comments will also be spotted by the big search engines like Google.

- Global reach – around 30 per cent of the membership comprises non-UK members. This has given rise to a number of regional clubs in locations such as Australia and Canada, as well as dozens of other countries spanning the world.

Another success story is that of US-based www.linkedin.com, a global two-million plus online networking community. It differs from other networks in that its orientation is much more business focused. If you go to the home page of Linkedin and click on 'View Case Studies', you will see the powerful evidence of its success at 'finding staff, finding jobs, making deals and finding experts'. Among its many helpful functions, the most exceptional is the superb 'Find Jobs' function. This shows your 'inside connections' to the job poster or company advertising the role. It's an excellent platform for developing a diverse professional network, and allows others to provide 'endorsements' of you, which are visible on your profile. Although the majority of members are US based, this network gives you access to a geographically diverse online business community comprising over 200,000 Britons, 75,000 Canadians, 40,000 Australians, 9,000 South Africans, 7,000 New Zealanders and hundreds of thousands from other countries across the globe.

More specialist networking platforms are continuously emerging. Examples are the Australian newcomers network (www.newcomersnetwork.com), a very useful resource and ready-made community designed to support those planning to move, or who have recently moved to Australia. There are others tailored to meet the needs of small businesses such as the Canada-based Business Partnerships (www.businesspartnerships.ca), which provide the following description as to what small business owners can achieve through membership of this network:

> *'meet other entrepreneurial individuals;*
>
> *get new ideas and perspectives;*
>
> *find services and products;*
>
> *learn what has worked for them in the past, and share your knowledge;*
>
> *partner in responding to a Request For Partners (RFP);*
>
> *sell your business-related products.*
>
> *You might be surprised to discover just how many people are willing to share their hard-won knowledge with you with no ulterior motives.'*

Basic or Guest membership tends to be provided on a free of charge basis on most sites, with the option of higher levels of functionality available for a modest subscription.

School friends, ex-colleagues and people research networks

Often with our 'heads down' focused on our current situation and priorities, we forget the strength of relationships we may have had with past work colleagues and past friends. Websites are now springing up all over the world to meet the current interest that people are showing in reviving old contacts. There are two sites in particular that we hear good reports about in terms of making useful work as well as social connections.

 *Friends Reunited (www.friendsreunited.co.uk)*

Over 12 million people in the UK have registered with this site for maintaining or re-establishing contact with schoolmates. Think how powerful the bond created by a shared 'heritage' of experiences at a highly impressionable age can be. Friends Reunited is a very powerful virtual meeting place to facilitate this. This is an extract from an email sent to us by a member. It is actually the story of a friend but is nonetheless inspiring and typical of the kind of useful work connections that this site can foster.

> *'Sally joined about 2 years ago and got in touch with an old school pal. She was a HR Manager but had previously been in retail, working her way up from Store Manager, District Manager, Training Manager into HR.*
>
> *They emailed several times over the next few months, relived memory lane and caught up on old acquaintances etc. My friend then had the offer of redundancy and let her friend Tom know. Before you know it, he had given her details of his friend who was looking for someone to work on*

a project who had HR and retail experience. Perfect match!! She has since moved to Canada and has a fabulous job as a consultant advising on Retail Training.'

As well as 40 people called David Beckham, Friends Reunited also boasts three million ex-work colleagues – but there is a better place for tracking these down…

 *Zoominfo (www.zoominfo.com)*

With its strapline 'people information summarised' Zoominfo is currently somewhat US biased in its 26-million person database. It does, however, provide high speed responses to UK, Australasian and European people searches for those millions who have any established 'web presence' (see chapter 10 E-connect with Magnetism).

Because of its sophisticated artificial intelligence, Zoominfo cleverly 'packages' such people's careers in a short biography, thereby providing an excellent research and pre-meeting preparation tool. For example, a senior manager client was very anxious about her forthcoming meeting with her CEO. She was daunted by his lofty position and was concerned that she did not know what on earth she might talk to him about to break the ice. Using Zoominfo, it took her less than 30 seconds to find out that he, like her, had previously been involved with the Massachusetts Institute of Technology (MIT). This piece of information helped significantly reduce her anxiety so that she could look forward more positively to the meeting. 'We shared our stories about MIT and got on like a house on fire' she reported after the meeting.

General search engines

Google is currently undeniably the leader in this field and the one that we find most people use.

'Bad news. No sign of them on Google', is what one partner at of one of the world's largest headhunting firms, said to Stuart about one of his clients. Stuart had hoped this client would be a serious contender for a senior post he was enquiring about. He was also told that a competing candidate had a very high profile on Google (see chapter 10 E-connect with magnetism for tips on getting spotted by search engines such as Google).

So keep checking your presence on Google as well as looking up other people. Nowadays, in an internet-focused world, web visibility reinforces credibility. You can speed up your chances of finding what you are looking for on Google by using the so-called 'advanced' search tools such as inverted commas around key words like names of people or topics.

Know how to make the most of chance meetings

The truth about networking is that it can happen anytime, anywhere. There is a time and a place for networking – it's called ANY time, and ANY place.

Scott Ginsberg, author of *The Power of Approachability* and a famous networking guru in the USA, makes sure this happens by wearing a badge with 'Scott' written on it all the time. He claims to have worn it every day since 2000. You may not wish to do the same but you should be aware that many of your best opportunities will come while you are engaged in everyday activities. Here is another incredible and inspiring story from one of Stuart's clients who is a director of a major global food business.

> *'I'd just popped out for a sandwich, and was on my way back to the office when I heard two chaps, who, like me were waiting to cross the road at the busy junction, having an animated conversation. "If only we had someone competent running IT" said one chap to the other. For some time I had been reflecting on how I felt at odds with my employers who were busy restructuring the business to meet the cost-cutting demands of the new owners. I was head of IT, and feeling frustrated at my unappreciated attempts to implement much-needed strategic change to enable the business to compete in a highly competitive environment. I knew I was very good at my job, and during quieter moments would remind myself of my talents, as if subconsciously preparing a pitch for a new employment opportunity. Girding my loins to seize this remarkable moment, I tapped the chap on the shoulder saying "Excuse me for butting in, but I'd very much like to talk to you about what you just said." Two months later I was heading up the European IT division of one of the world's largest food businesses. That was six years ago – and I've loved every minute!'*

It took a good deal of confidence and a great elevator pitch to make this tap on the shoulder. You may not be quite ready to do this, but what you can do is make sure that you are on the look-out for these kinds of opportunities and ensure that you are prepared to make the best of them by, for example, making sure that you have:

- your excellent business cards at the ready (pages 121–2)

- your address book or an electronic means of beaming information (pages 244–5) about a possibly useful contact
- a well-practised elevator pitch (pages 114–20)
- a way of making your name memorable (pages 114)
- interesting small talk stories (pages 128–9) to proactively start conversations
- plenty of generosity to spare – doing a small favour, such as moving your position to make room or helping someone lift luggage on to a train can trigger opportunities
- an approachable appearance and a readiness to enjoy yourself (pages 113–14).

There is little point, however, in doing all this preparation and having fun with your new contact if you don't follow up a chance meeting promptly – an email or phone call within 48 hours is what power networkers recommend. But don't forget that all this advice will have a better chance of working if you made the meeting enjoyable in the first place:

> *'The most important take-away from a chance meeting is not what you both said but how you both felt. People remember meetings they enjoyed.'*
>
> Juliet Erickson, *The Art of Persuasion*

15

Know the secrets of efficiency

Business card management

DOES THIS EXTRACT FROM A *Financial Times* article (24 January 2005) by Lucy Kellaway, ring bells for you?

> *'The whole networking process defeats me, in particular the business cards. I keep my own at the bottom of my handbag, and they are usually a bit grubby on the rare occasions I am required to produce one. Other people's cards go back into my bag, and get fished out whenever I spring clean it. They then sit on my desk for a while before eventually going into the bin.'*

If it does, it shouldn't (say we from our pristine high horses!). Seriously, very few of us manage the task of card management as we would like to. But you may like to know a few tips from those who do it better than most.

The first is to be strictly selective. You have to decide upon your own specific rules, which will vary according to your objectives. But, generally speaking, it is good to only keep the ones that immediately appear to have some relevance to your work needs or the ones from people you found interesting and fun to be with.

Everyone recommends carrying a separate 'Inbox' and an 'Outbox' for cards. Your own cards should be in a smart card container. Other people's cards should be in a different container – but equally smart looking. (People are often very proud of their cards and like to see them treated with respect.)

When you get home or back to the office, file them immediately. As you do so, mark each with some key memory-jogging words.

How and where you store your cards will depend partly on your budget and partly on your innate preferences. Although you can now buy sophisticated electronic scanners, which will enable you to store your data quickly on your computer, many people prefer to stick to tried-and-tested methods. Many people still use physical card storage systems, such as Rolodex. There are many varieties of these available from office supplies companies.

You must then choose how you are going to file the cards in alphabetical order. Will you use the name of the person or their company or their profession? You can choose any as long as you are consistent. Sometimes it may be a good idea to file people in several places. You can use blank cards to do this with the person's name and a note where the original card is filed written on them.

It is often helpful to further categorise contacts into A, 'hot' (of immediate/short-term interest); B, 'warm' (of medium-term interest); and C, 'potentials' (of longer-term interest). This helps you to prioritise ongoing contact maintenance. This kind of categorisation is made far easier on an electronic database as might be available on a computer programme of your PC or handheld unit such as a Palm Pilot. Many of these also offer remote 'beaming', which means that contact details (including straplines!) can be exchanged electronically in less than a second. This is a great time saver at networking events and chance meetings. It also saves you entering the data later and will ensure (for those of us who mistype regularly) that the data is entered correctly.

 *Review and update your data*

Whatever storage method you use, it is important to freshen up your contact list every six months. This is especially true if you have decided to build a 'quality' network as opposed to one that has many thousands of contacts (see pages 186–8).

In their book *Make Your Business Click: How to Value and Grow Your Network*, Teten, Fisher and Allen introduce a formula, based on their research, to help assess the value of your network. If you are not mathematically inclined, simply think about the value of each contact, in terms of the three components the authors used to develop their formula. These are:

- relevance of the other person to your current objectives
- strength of the relationship in terms of degree of trust
- credibility of the person.

Use a pre-event checklist

Louis Pasteur suggested that 'Fortune favours the prepared mind.' It is so easy in an over-pressurised world to rush off to meetings and events without doing sufficient preparation. Having a ready-prepared checklist before events can be a great support. You will need to make your own so that it is relevant for you and the kind of events you attend, but here are some suggestions of questions that you might want to include:

- Have you eaten? Arriving at an event hungry is not a good idea. Your mind will be on the buffet and not the conversation (especially if it is looking 'thin' as they often do!). It is also a good deal easier to exchange cards and other information if you do not have to balance a plate as well as a glass.
- Have you done relevant research regarding the event (such as last year's summary or paper), the organisers, the speakers and other potentially interesting attendees? This is all straightforward and relatively simple to do nowadays thanks to the likes of Google.
- Have you thought of some conversation starters (including your purpose for attending the event) and a memory story for your name?
- Have you enough cards (and some blank ones too for others who have forgotten or run out of cards)? Are your card holders both looking smart and polished if they are silver?
- Have you got a memo pad and pen?
- Have you got a spare name badge for yourself in case the organisers have missed you out or misrepresented your

details? (These should look professional and be easily readable for people with poor eyesight. They can include an appealing strapline as well as your name. So many people are now using these all the time.)

- Are you wearing or carrying a potential 'talking point'?
- Have you got your address book or electronic organiser?
- Is your phone switched on to divert mode?
- Have you done some relaxation and positive thinking exercises?
- Have you had a wash and brush up?

16

Know how to help others

VERY FEW EXPERIENCES ARE MORE confidence building than helping others surmount their fears and hang-ups. Having read this book and hopefully increased your confidence as a result, you are in a good position to help others. The more people who are confidently networking in the world, the better it will be for all of us. What a waste of talent and opportunity if people sit on information just because they haven't enough confidence to share it. This quote from Professor Herminia Ibarra of INSEAD confirms our own beliefs and conclusions drawn from our experiences:

> *'I have one thing to pass on about "confident networking" – when you are confident you think you can contribute a lot to others, and therefore, you don't think you are wasting their time or "using them" in any way because you know you have valuable information and resources. Ironically, confidence makes the principle of reciprocity come alive.'*

Reciprocity, as we have indicated several times in this book, is a core principle of networking. By helping others in your organisation to become more confident, you will be not just doing a great favour to them but also to the network in general and therefore indirectly to you as well.

Coach rather than lecture

Hopefully this is just a reminder. Most of us know that the best learning takes place when people are encouraged and coaxed to discover and learn rather than just being advised and taught. Of course there is a place for passing on information directly, especially when speed is essential, but if you are trying to build someone's confidence, it is much better to take the shorter route and adopt a coaching style. But we are all human and when the obvious answer is staring us in the face, it can be hard to hold back the sermon. Here are some examples of questions you could use that might be more helpful than just telling others what they 'ought to do'. You could copy a few of them out and read them to yourself just before meeting up with a colleague or member of staff whose confidence you know needs an encouraging boost.

- What would you like to achieve?
- What do you want to gain from being more assertive?
- What stops you from approaching people you want to connect with?
- What would be the benefits of making a direct approach to the leader herself?
- What have you done already?

- Where or with whom does this occur most frequently?
- Is there anyone you could use as a role model to inspire you?
- What are you missing out on by holding back and not joining conversations or lunching on your own?
- When you are feeling confident how do you tackle people like this?
- If you had all the confidence in the world, what would you say?
- What do you need to do differently?
- How could you overcome these?
- How will you monitor your progress?
- What would be a realistic (but challenging) date for review?
- What is a small, achievable step you could take at the next meeting?

Also, point them in the direction of this book!

Below is a list of some frequently expressed fears and anxieties. Beside each we have included a reference to the section in the book that will help you to help them. Alternatively, you could of course also think about buying them their own personal copy of this book and insert a few markers in the appropriate place. (That's one of the best tips in this book!)

'Everyone else was in animated conversation' (page 132)

'I didn't want to leave her stranded' (pages 47–61)

'I can't remember names' (pages 138–9)

'I'm a very private person' (pages 200–11)

'I don't want to use people' (pages 47–61)

'It feels so cold and calculating' (pages 13–27 and 75–80)

'I'm too self-conscious. I think everyone is looking at me' (pages 31–46)

'I can never get past the secretaries' (pages 200–11)

'I don't have any contacts to help others' (pages 18–19 and 229–43)

'I don't like flashy business cards' (pages 121–2)

'I'm out of work – I don't know how to respond when people ask what I do' (pages 37–40 and 114–20)

'I talk too much when I am nervous' (pages 93–102)

'I want to make contact, but I haven't been in touch with them for over five years' (pages 93–102 and 183–99)

'Approaching others is not my style. I'm too introverted' (pages 1–27)

'I'm not really good at selling myself' (pages 105–24)

17

Know how to encourage your organisations to be better connected

HERE'S SOME BAD NEWS – YOU cannot expect any organisation you work in to make it easy for you to network. We are giving it to you straight knowing that with your new improved confidence bad news shouldn't daunt you for long!

Networking, as you know, is a long-term strategy so it is rarely given much priority by organisations. Increased competition and an unsteady economic climate often lead to short-term thinking and a fire-fighting management style. Even if you head up your own small business or are a sole trader, you may find it difficult for yourself for much the same reasons! There will always appear to be something more urgent to do than network for the sake of networking alone. This is understandable but not acceptable. For your own career's sake you need to be operating in an environment that is as networking-friendly as it can be. But that will not be a good enough argument for the boss.

So you may have to convince and keep on convincing the powers that be (even if they are you!) of the benefits of networking, not just to you but the organisation as a whole. Culture cascades from the top so the senior people in any organisation, small or large, must be committed and, ideally, be excellent role models.

But arguing your case will rarely be enough; you will need to be proactive. This may involve making specific suggestions and kick-starting projects that will help you and others to keep networking. You will also need to have the courage to criticise. Many organisations, having heard abut the wonders of networking, pay lip-service to ideas and agree to token projects. For example, a manager might agree to a short talk on the subject at the annual conference or allow one person to leave work early each month to attend a networking event. Welcome though they may be, neither of these initiatives will make an appreciable difference to most organisations. (Though they may sound good when the manager is having his annual review!)

We hope these tips will give you some ideas about how to confidently and competently approach this issue.

Tips for encouraging your organisation to be better connected

 *Read the research and gurus*

If you are going to argue the case for networking, you need to back it up with data that will impress those in positions of power. Keep an eye out for articles and new impressive statistics in the journals and on the web. For example, Stuart recently published an article entitled 'The Networked Organisation' for *CriticalEYE*, the publication of the European Centre for Strategic Thought Leadership. See also the Recommended Books list on pages 272–3. We would particularly recommend you look at two books on this subject. The first is by two leading-edge experts in knowledge management and social capital, Don Cohen and Larry Prusak, authors of *In Good Company: How Social Capital Makes Organisations Work*. They argue convincingly that 'the smart organisation understands that human capital can only be fully optimised if people belong to networks where they can co-ordinate and amplify their necessarily limited knowledge.' The second is by Rob Cross and Andrew Parker and is entitled *The Hidden Power of Social Networks: Understanding How Work Really Gets Done in Organisations*. This is packed with data from a major ongoing research project they initiated. Here are a few quotes from their book which we hope will whet your appetite and demonstrate some of the persuasive material it contains:

> *'What distinguished high performers were larger and more diversified networks.'*
>
> *'We find a comparative lack of connectivity among those lower in the hierarchy.'*
>
> *'Leaders can quickly create networks that are overly dependent on them.'*
>
> *'Almost universally, people reported that their most valued information relationships had connected on issues outside work.'*
>
> *'Unless we are forced to interact with people different from ourselves, there is an extremely strong tendency, known as homophily, for us to seek out those who are similar.'*

Suggest that the networks within your organisation are analysed

This is particularly important for large organisations. There are now tools that can be used to make this task much easier and more efficient. They will identify who connects most with whom and where there are gaps and bottlenecks in the network. The results can be produced in easy-to-read illustrations of the web of connections. This may attract more attention from managers and other leaders who are tired of looking at conventional data.

There are a number of organisations who produce analysis software and offer a consulting service. Two that we recommend who do this work are:

- Rob Cross, based in the USA, produces Social Network Analysis software – www.robcross.org
- Fourgroups, based in London, provide a simple formula for mapping out the people networks in your organisation, and can recommend changes to optimise these – www.fourgroups.com

If your organisation is very small you may be able to collect some data and make a simple drawing yourself. Even if your 'research' isn't perfect, it may get everyone at least thinking and talking about networking.

Encourage appropriate company blogging

The volume of blogs is exploding so fast that it is difficult to keep up to date with the figures. The latest we have are:

100,000 in March 2003 to 9,000,000 in April 2005 (*Business Week*, 2 May 2005).

One of the reasons for the rapid increase is that a growing number of large firms have now realised the power of blogging and have created their own online discussion areas to promote it. When Bob Lutz, vice-chairman of General Motors launched his FastLane Blog (http://fastlane.gmblogs.com/), he was instantly flooded with suggestions and complaints, and was applauded by car buffs for his balanced responses. Similarly, Microsoft and Sun Microsystems are now very happy to have their subject matter experts take to blogging.

But, a word of warning if you do decide to blog about your company. There have been some recent cases of employees being fired for doing so in a way that was considered defamatory. So, check if your company has codes of conduct on blogging. Some do not. For example, Microsoft encourages employees to stay connected to customers through blogs, but it doesn't have a corporate policy on blogging. Microsoft spokesman Adam Sohn is quoted in the above edition of *Business Week* as saying:

> *'We see blogging as a great opportunity for direct and deep two-way conversations with the online community. We get important, real-time feedback on our products, and customers get greater insight to what is going on with key technologies inside the company, which helps them plan their business and continue to be successful. Today, there are more than 1,000 bloggers at Microsoft, and that number keeps growing. These [bloggers] are, by and large, the domain experts in their areas, and as a company full of people passionate about technology, the overall belief is that people will do the right thing.'*

 *Bombard the training department with requests*

Not quite literally, of course! But remember that it may take a substantial amount of nagging to ensure opportunities for networking make their priority list. These departments, especially if they are overloaded and underfinanced, don't always share the information that they are sent on conferences, meetings, new networking organisations and training programmes. You may have to seek out this information yourself and present it to them again – and again!

You could also make suggestions of people you think will bring a fresh approach from 'the outside world' into your organisation as speakers, consultants or trainers.

 *Write reports on your networking events*

Much of your networking may have to take place out of office hours and even be financed by you. Let your organisation know what you are doing. Giving them regular summaries of speakers' talks, breakfast briefings and feedback on the valuable contacts you made, will arouse interest. You can do this through newsletters or even the local press and business magazines. Some editors welcome this kind of feedback on events from people on the 'coalface' more than that from journalists. If it is obvious that these events were enjoyable and successful for you, envy might work in your favour and attract some others to join you.

Encourage mentoring schemes

These are not just a great way of learning and sharing good practice, they are good for networking too. It is yet another way to share contacts both inside and outside the organisation.

Use your legs

Although sending an email to a colleague in the next-door department might be quicker than walking with a message, it may do little to strengthen the relationship. Also, suggesting to a colleague that you walk upstairs together rather than taking the lift, might give you a chance to 'small talk' yourselves into a networking relationship. (Most people know for health reasons that it is good to do this and will thank you for prodding their conscience – a good start!)

18

Know how to keep learning

KEEP READING – WE DON'T MAKE any claim to this being the only book on networking or confidence building that you will ever need. On the contrary. We believe that you will benefit greatly from reading many other books on both subjects. We have included a selection of books we think could be helpful in Appendix 2. But there are many others that might be just as useful to you. So keep checking the bookstores and the internet for new books and articles. Most journals and magazines now have websites and publish some of their articles electronically.

Find more training in networking and confidence

As with any form of interactive training, we recommend that you base your decision on the provider on the quality of the individuals who will be delivering the training. A search on the internet will reveal many companies. Most of these we do not have any feedback on. We have, however, heard excellent reports about the quality of training offered by the following:

- Management Advantage (http://www.manadvan.com/) provide Networking, Negotiation and Body Language courses that receive very positive feedback.
- Toastmasters (http://www.toastmasters.org/) provide training in Networking Communication Skills, and specialise in public speaking.

If you are looking for more training specifically in Confident Networking, we highly recommend you check out: http://www.confidentnetworking.com! Both face-to-face individual coaching and company training programmes, as well as internet-based services can be provided.

19

Know how to network strategically

Make a personal action plan

AFTER READING THIS BOOK WE suggest that you create an action plan for yourself to improve your networking skills. The most useful and motivating way to do this is to choose a real-life work dream on which to focus your goals. This will help ensure that networking doesn't slip down the priority list, as it has a tendency to do. Below is an example of a model you can use as a guide. You will see that we have also linked the goals to the qualities, skills and knowledge that we have recommended you develop in order to become a more confident networker. These would be the ones you have chosen to build and they will therefore differ from those in our example.

You will also note that the goals are very specific and that the action plan has some clear target dates. But the good news is that there are rewards as well! If you can, why not try to make these useful as we have done in our example.

Finally, remember, this action plan is not a business or project plan. You will almost certainly need one of these as well. This one should be specifically aimed at building up your confidence in your networking ability, though indirectly it will also, of course, help you achieve success in your chosen work goal.

Example of confident networking action plan

My Personal Vision Statement

I would like to launch my own specialist travel consultancy by next summer.

	Short-term Confident Networking goals	**Target date: 31 March**
☐	My Reward: new handheld computer	(, chapter 5)
☐	Check and reinforce my current connections to see who I know who may have some knowledge or contacts	(, chapter 15; , chapter 11)
☐	Seek out at least 6 new contacts with people who choose holidays with a difference	(, chapter 14)
☐	Write 3 weblogs that will prompt sharing of information on specialist travel	(, chapter 10)
☐	Attend at least 3 relevant conferences, seminars or briefings	(, chapter 7; , chapter 13)
☐	Rehearse my conversation skills	(, chapter 9)
☐	Find an inspiring mentor to keep me motivated	(, chapter 6)
☐	Talk about travel in different places such as the Nail Bar with strangers	(, chapter 7 and , chapter 9)
☐	Clarify my strengths and appeal	(, chapter 2)

Medium-term Confident Networking goals	**Target date: 30 September**
☐ My Reward: course of massage sessions	(, chapter 5)
☐ Review my contact list and prioritise	(, chapter 15)
☐ Clarify what I will need help with and make approaches	(, chapter 6)
☐ Have focus group with key contacts to help me decide which specialist areas to focus on	(, chapter 11)
☐ Clarify my operating principles and establish code of conduct	(, chapter 3)
☐ Compose and rehearse elevator pitch	(, chapter 8)
☐ Offer free holiday to two contacts willing to test out holiday and make connections in chosen areas	(, chapter 5; , chapter 14)
☐ Take test holiday alone and talk, talk to everyone	(, chapter 7; , chapter 9)
☐ Start language course	(, chapter 2; , chapters 14 & 18)

Long-term Confident Networking goals	**Target date: 31 January**
☐ My Reward: professional makeover for my office	(, chapter 5)
☐ Choose key colours, strapline and get impactful business stationery printed	(, chapter 13)
☐ Reorganise my contact list and make specific one for this business	(, chapter 15)
☐ Set monthly lunch/drinks dates in diary for maintaining contact in key relationships	(, chapter 11)
☐ Speak at 3 events	(, chapter 13)
☐ Write an article for travel magazine	(, chapter 13)
☐ Use my connections to find someone to help me with business plan	(, chapter 14)

- [ ] Launch website with forum (🐝, chapters 10 & 13)
- [ ] Practise assertive skills to help deal with possible cynics (🐝, chapter 12)
- [ ] Get help in assessing my progress and make new action plan (🦉, chapter 19)

Create extra time

None of the above will happen unless you clear a space in your diary to ensure that it does. This means that you will have to cut down or stop doing a number of other activities. Take five minutes to decide which these are the moment you have written your action plan – or, why not right now!

Review your action plan and check that you have allocated yourself sufficient hours. Remember that being and looking relaxed and in control is essential in confident networking. So, set inspiring challenges but always allow yourself plenty of recovery time as well.

. . . And finally

We hope you have enjoyed this book and that it will help you to network with increased confidence. Writing it has been an exciting adventure for us. Through doing it we have met some remarkable people who have generously shared their wisdom. We have also 'met' each other in a different way. Our fears about working together proved totally unfounded. Indeed, we are now looking forward with enthusiasm to writing this book's companion volume.

When we first set off we were unsure of exactly where the journey would take us. We knew there was a problem and we were sure that together we could make a contribution to solving it. We did not know how that would happen but we did believe it would! And, we knew we had the drive. We could not stand by and watch so many talented but unconfident people miss out on the networking 'revolution'.

Now that we have finished and look back, our journey appears so straightforward and the solutions relatively simple. We hope that this is exactly how you will feel when you have fully completed the programme. Confident networking is not difficult. As we said earlier, you just need to know what to do, when to do it and have the courage to test out the strategies step by step. Trust that one day it will suddenly 'click into place'. It will have started to feel natural and so easy – just like it does to those super-confident people you admired earlier. But we are trusting that when it does, you will never take your confidence for granted. You must continue to care for it, especially when it has been dealt a knock. We also hope that you too will be committed to helping others build their confidence. In networking, we all lose out if people with potential are needlessly held back.

Finally, we hope to have a chance of connecting with you either face to face at one of our events or 'virtually' through our website www.confidentnetworking.com We would especially love to hear any inspiring stories you may have to tell. Good luck!

Notes

1. 'Inhibiting and Facilitating Conditions of the Human Smile: A Non-Obtrusive Test of the Facial Feedback Hypothesis', F. Strack, L.L. Martin and S. Stepper, *Journal of Personality and Social Psychology*, 54, no. 5 (1988):768–777
2. 'Self Disclosure and Liking: A Meta-Analytical Review', N.L. Collins and L.C. Miller, *Psychological Bulletin*, 116, no. 3 (1994): 457–475
3. 'Suggestopedia, Biofeedback and the Search for the Alpha State, W. Jane Bancroft', *Journal of Accelerated Learning and Teaching*, Vol. 22, Issues 1 and 2, 1997
4. 'References and measures of nonverbal behaviour', 1969 *Behavior Research Methods and Instrumentation, 1,* 203–207.

Appendix 1: Useful websites

The following organisations function as powerful networking platforms for their members. We know of many people who have both enhanced their expertise and found extremely useful contacts at many of these institutions.

British Computer Society
http://bcs.org
Industry body for IT professionals

British Hospitality Association
http://www.bha-online.org.uk
A major trade association for the catering industry

British Printing Industrial Federation
http://www.britishprint.com
Trade association for those working in print and graphic design

Chartered Insurance Institute
http://www.cii.co.uk
Professional association for those working in insurance and financial services

Chartered Institute of Logistics and Transport
http://www.ciltuk.org.uk
The professional body for transport, logistics and integrated supply-chain management

Chartered Institute of Marketing
http://www.cim.co.uk
Professional body for those involved in marketing

Chartered Institute of Personnel and Development
http://www.cipd.co.uk
Professional body for those involved in the management and development of people

Chartered Institute of Purchasing and Supply
http://www.cips.org
Professional body representing purchasing and supply chain professionals

Institute of Chartered Accountants in England and Wales
http://www.icaew.co.uk
Europe's largest professional accountancy body

Institute of Electrical Engineers
http://www.iee.org
Europe's largest professional engineering body covering IT, engineering, electronics, power and communications

Institute of Financial Services
http://ifslearning.com
A leading body for the provision of both education and life-long career support services to the financial services industry

Institute of Risk Management
http://theirm.org
Professional body for risk management professionals

Institute of Sales and Marketing Management
http://www.ismm.co.uk
UK professional body for those involved in sales and marketing

International Customer Service Association
http://icsa.com
Promotes the development and awareness of the customer service profession through networking, education and research

Law Society of England and Wales
http://www.lawsociety.org.uk
The regulatory and representative body for solicitors in England and Wales

Project Management Institute
http://www.pmi.org
Support for project management professionals worldwide

Telecomms Industrial Association
http://www.tia.org.uk
Provider of support for companies involved in telecommunications products or services

Entrepreneurs organisations

Business Link
www.businesslink.gov.uk
This a national support network managed by the Department of Trade and Industry providing practical advice for small business start-ups, and, especially through its local training events, provides excellent networking opportunities. Business Link has an extensive network of regional locations

Innovateur
www.innovateur.co.uk
This is a very helpful resource giving information about free events around the UK, the majority organised in conjunction with leading business schools

Chambers of Commerce
www.chambersonline.co.uk
Promoting the voice of local business communities around the UK. Over 200,000 business people attended British Chambers of Commerce networking events in 2004. There are over 45 regional chambers in the UK

Special interest networks

It is good to 'network to your interests'. We know a number of success stories arising from networking in organisations that play to your passion. The London Sustainability Exchange is a great example of such a network for Londoners interested in the environment: http://www.lsx.org.uk

Also, the Women in Technology International Network http://www.witi.com is a platform for women, providing connections, resources and opportunities in the technology field.

Appendix 2: Recommended books

Networking skills

Network Your Way to Success, John Timperley, Piatkus, 2002. ISBN 0 7499 2283 4

Dig Your Well Before You're Thirsty, Harvey Mackay, Random House, 1997. ISBN 0 3854 8546 8

The Networking Survival Guide, Diane Darling, McGraw-Hill, 2003. ISBN 0 0714 0999 8

Networking – The art of making friends, Carole Stone, Vermilion, 2001. ISBN 0 0918 5711 2

Personal Networking, Mick Cope, FT Prentice Hall, 2003. ISBN 0 2736 6359 3

Power Networking, Donna Fisher and Sandy Vilas, Mountain Harbour Publications, 1991. ISBN 0 9627 8254 8

Research and science of networks

Linked – The New Science of Networks, Albert-Laszlo Barabasi, Perseus Publishing, 2002. ISBN 0 7382 0667 9

Reinventing Your Career

Working Identity, Herminia Ibarra, Harvard Business School Press, 2003. ISBN 1 5913 9413 9

Networking for Organisations

Connections, Lee Sproull and Sara Kiesler, The MIT Press, 1991. ISBN 0 2621 9306 X

The Hidden Power of Social Networks, Rob Cross and Andrew Parker, Harvard Business School Press, 2004. ISBN 1 5913 9270 5

In Good Company: How Social Capital Makes Organisations Work, Don Cohen and Larry Prusak, Harvard Business School Press, 2001. ISBN 0 8758 4913 X

E-networking

Networking for Life, Thomas Power, Ecademy Press, 2003. ISBN 0 9545 0930 7

How to 'read' other people

The Book of Tells, Peter Collett, Bantam Books, 2003. ISBN 0 5538 1459 1

Personal development – confidence building

Self Esteem, Gael Lindenfield, Thorsons, 2000. ISBN 0 7223 4007 8

Assert Yourself, Gael Lindenfield, Thorsons, 2000. ISBN 0 0071 2345 0

Super Confidence, Gael Lindenfield, Thorsons, 2000. ISBN 0 7225 4011 6

Self Esteem Bible, Gael Lindenfield, Thorsons, 2004. ISBN 0 0071 7955 3

Appendix 3: UAP form

1. Innate aptitudes	Appeal factor	Potentially interested parties

2. Developed character strengths	Appeal factor	Potentially interested parties

3. Technical expertise	Appeal factor	Potentially interested parties

4. People skills	Appeal factor	Potentially interested parties

Index

Note: page numbers in **bold** refer to diagrams.

49–1 rule 77

action plans 261–4
advice giving 88
affirmations 100–1
Allen, Scott 97, 124, 186
alumni organisations 233
ambition 24
analytical personalities 42
approachability 113–14
aptitudes 37, 38
arrogance 81–2, 84–5, 92
assertiveness 21–2, 58–9
lack of 68
self-protection and 199–211
assessing network skills 6–8
Aurora 185, 196
Australian newcomers network 237
authenticity 57–9
availability 90

Bacheler, Mike 127
Barker, Simon 221–2
'beaming' 242, 245
benefits of networking 22–7
big picture thinking 156
'blast-mailing' 170
'blogging' 173–6, 255–6
body language 112–14, 134–6, 144, 159–60
Branson, Richard 22
Buggy, Cheryl 139
business cards 121–3, 139, 169–70, 242–6
business lunches 230
Business Week (magazine) 173–4, 256
Buzzy Bee Skills *see* confidence, outer

Canada-based Business Partnerships 237
career direction 23
career insurance 26–7, 232
case studies
drive 62–3
e-networking 163
first impressions 106–7, 115–16
integrity 50–2
reputation 213, 225
self-belief 33–4, 41–2
Central Stagers 108
challenges, constructive 157
chambers of commerce 17, 223
chance encounters 105–7, 115–16, 240–2
charitable projects 25, 233–4
chat rooms 175–6
clarification 89, 208–9
clothing 111–12
clubs 223, 224–5, 233, 235
co-operation 158
coaching others 249–51
codes
of ethics 53–6, 173
moral 49–50, 202–3
Cohen, Don 254
colour, use of 217
Commercial Cross-over Scripts 150–6
community involvement 233
competitors 217
compliments 85, 193–4
composure 113
confidence 4, 8, 12
definition 18–22
exudation 124
inner 9–10, 21–2, 29–102
and courage 93–102
and drive 62–74
and generosity 75–80
and humility 81–92
and integrity 47–61
and self-belief 31–46
inspiring in others 79
outer 10–11, 22, 103–225
and assertiveness 199–211
and building and maintaining relationships 182–98
and conversation skills 125–61
and e-networking 161–82
and first impressions 105–24
and reputation 212–25
and social skills 32
visualisations for 21
Confidence Club, The 3–4
Confident Networking 260, 266
conversation skills 41–2, 125–61
and body language 134–5, 136, 144, 159–60
breaking into groups 132–3
Commercial Cross-over Scripts 150–6
danger areas 143–4, 158–60
guide to 155–61
levels of conversation 127–32
and listening skills 32, 77–8, 130, 133–7
maintaining familiarity 131–2
and memory 138–40
polite probing 130
qualities of good conversations 126
questioning techniques 130, 145–51

and selective self-disclosure 129
and self belief 132
sentence fillers 158
small talk 128–9, 140–4, 188, 242, 246
testing for trust 130–1, 189–90
tips 132–7
tone of voice 144–5, 160
Cool Cat Qualities *see* confidence, inner
Cope, Nick 75
courage 42, 93–102
creative visualisation 65–7
criminal networks 48–9
criticism 54, 159
Cross, Rob 24, 76, 186, 254, 255
cross-cultural networking 122, 195–6
Cross-over Scripts, Commercial 150–6
curriculum vitae (CV) 32
customer base expansion 24–5
Cybaea 174
cynicism 200

Darling, Diane 179
decisiveness 157
defining networking 13–27
Department of Trade and Industry (DTI) 25
de-stressing techniques 87
diagnostic responses 156
direct language 157, 202
direction 157
disagreements 203
disappointment 69
discussion forums 161, 168, 175–6, 236
dogsbodies 219
drive 62–74
building and maintaining 65–74
case study 62–3
and down-times 63–4
Dunbar, Thomas 186

e-networking 161–81
case study 163
using email 161, 163–4, 167–70
false sense of security regarding 164–6
fears regarding 98
on-line business cards for 169–70
and online social networking platforms 234–40
profiles for 170–1, 187, 235
tips for 166–81
e-visibility 171–2
Ecademy 3–4, 53, 77, 173, 184, 201, 225, 235–6
efficiency 243–7
elevator pitches 115–20, 171, 241–2
email 161, 163–4, 167–70
emotional punch-bags 200
emotions 157–8
endorphins 66, 73
energy 70–1, 120
Englehard, Allan 174
entertainment 69, 192
envy 67–8
Erickson, Juliet 197–8, 242
escape routes 102, 154–5
see also 'get lost lines'
ethics 156, 202
codes of 53–6, 173
events, preparation for 246–7
exaggeration 85
extroverts 4, 18–20, 140–1
eye contact 135, 159

failures 69
families 49, 196–7
favours, cheeky 200
fears 96–9, 100–1, 250–1
feedback 36, 88, 113
Feiner, Michael 101
'fight or flight' response 205
first impressions 105–24
and body language 112–14
and business cards 121–3
case studies of 106–7, 115–16
checklist for 111
and clothing 111–12
conveying passion and 120
and e-networking 166–7, 172
exercise for 109–10
and image 108–10
and name badges 121
and names 114
and positive personal pitches 114–20
talking points and 124, 247
first moves, making 188
Fisher, Donna 186
'flaming' 165
'Fogging' 209
Fourgroups 255
friends, taking along for support 101
Friends Reunited 238–9

generosity 75–80, 242
'get lost lines' 197–8
ghost writers 222
Gilbert, David 25
Ginsberg, Scott 240
global connections 236–7
goals 83–4, 262–4
Google (search engine) 240
gossip 209–10
Graham, Simon 176
greetings cards 180–1, 192
gut feelings 141

hairdressers 234
'halo' effect 162
hand gestures 114
health clubs 233
help, asking for 89–91
helping others 248–51
homeostasis principle 107–8
honesty 42, 54, 57
HTML (hypertext mark-up language) 177
humility 43, 81–92, 158, 196
humour 43, 196

Ibarra, Herminia 23, 213–14, 232, 248
image 108–10, 166–7, 217
inspiration 157
instinct 141
integrity 47–61
affronts to 50
case study of 50–2
maintenance 53–61
and owning up to your mistakes 60

integrity – *continued*
  and passing on contacts 59–60
  questioning your 52–3
  and selling mode 60–1
  and trust 47–50
internet 17, 33, 161
  see also e-networking
introverts 4, 20, 140
intuition 141–2
investors 25–6

Jennings, Marilyn 24
jobs, new 23
journalists 219–22
journals 36, 254
judgements 141

Kellaway, Lucy 243
kindness 54
knocks, recovering from 43–6
knowledge base 11, 227–66
  efficiency 243–7
  helping others 248–51
  life-long learning 259–60
  organisational connectivity 252–8
  strategic networking 261–4
  where to connect 229–42

learned responses 156
learning, life-long 91–2, 259–60
leisure activities 69, 192
Lichtenberg, Ronna 232
likeability 37–8, 88
Lindsay, Hugh 145
Linkedin 236
listening skills 32, 77–8, 130, 133–7
live events 236
locations for networking 229–42
logos 177
Long, Giles 94–5
long-term outlook 74
Lopata, Andy 152–3
Lutz, Bob 256

Mackay, Harvey 75, 190, 231–2
Mafia 48–9
mail 180–1, 192
Management Advantage 260
Mandela, Nelson 96
martyrs 80
media, dealing with 219–22
memory 138–40
mentors 258
Microsoft 256
mistakes, owning up to 60
modelling behaviour 35, 67–8
moods, enhancing 218–19
Moore, Mary Tyler 101
moral codes 49–50, 202–3
moral dilemmas 57, 190
motivation 157
  see also drive

nail bars 234
name badges 121, 246–7
names
  making your own memorable 114, 242, 246
  remembering 138–9
needs, other people's 77–8, 153, 248–51
negativity
  isolating yourself from 68–9
  watchdogs for 72–4
netiquette 165, 169, 173
networking nodes 218
networking organisations 17, 184
networking trees **16**, 18, **19**
Nevin, Mike 26
new businesses 25
new jobs 23
news 69, 193
no, being able to say 58

Olivier, Laurence 120
open-mindedness 54
organisational connectivity 252–8
Osei-Kwaku, Larry 225
other people
  helping 248–51
  inspiring confidence in 79
  making them feel small 200
  needs of 77–8, 153, 248–51
  worrying about their opinions 87–8
outsiders, feeling like 89

parent associations 233
Parker, Andrew 24, 76, 186, 254
parties 224
passing on contacts 59–60, 76, 77, 79
passion 120, 153
Pasteur, Louis 246
people skills 38, 40
perfectionism 81–2
persistence 42
personal appeal 37–8, 88
personal branding 214–17
personal space 114, 160
personal strengths 37, 39, 41–3
phoney people 34
photographs 171, 177
physical disabilities 43, 94–5
physical fitness 70–1
pitches 114–20
  elevator 115–20, 171, 241–2
pleasurable work 70
politeness 54
positivity
  and attitudes 221
  conveyance 157
  and moods 218–19
  and personal pitches 114–20
  and self-talk 100–1
  and visualisation 65–7, 155–6
postcards 192
posture 113, 134–7, 160
Power, Penny 201
Power, Thomas 26, 77, 80, 185
pre-interview information 220
'predators' 199–209
prejudice 192
presentations 222–3
press releases 220
pride 158
principles 156
priorities 157
proactivity 156–7, 220, 253
professional associations 230–1

profiles, e-networking 170–1, 187, 235
promotion 23–4
Prusak, Larry 254
psychology 194–5
put-downs, dealing with 204–5
putting people at ease 141

quality of relationships 185–7
quantity of relationships 185–7
questions 130, 145–51
  coping with unwelcome 149–50
  Directive (closed) 61, 147–8
  Hypothetical 148–9
  Leading 148
  Open-ended 146
  Reflective 146–7

rapport building 188–9
rationality 202
re-phrasing 137
reality checks 92
receiving 75
reciprocity 248–9
redundancy 32, 62–3, 213
reflection 135, 146–7
reframing 73–4
relationship building and maintenance 13–14, 182–98
  quality versus quantity 185–7
  tips for 187–98
report writing 257
reputation 212–25
  building 214–25
  case studies of 213, 225
researching contacts 101–2, 143, 187, 230, 239, 246
respect 47, 202
responsibility 156
rewarding yourself 71–2, 78–9
risk-taking 94–100, 102
role-models 67–8
Rolodexes 244–5
ruthlessness 200

Salk, Jonas 101
school friends 238–9
Schwartz, David 188
scripts
  Commercial Cross-over 150–6
  for dealing with 'predators' 205–8
search engines 177, 240
self-belief 31–46
  and accepting and dealing with weaknesses 41–3
  case studies of 33–4, 41–2
  and conversation skills 132
  developing 34–8
  and playing too safe 31
  and processing written information 32–3
  and recovering from knocks 43–6
  and seizing the moment 33
  and selling yourself short 31–2
  and social skills 32
  and unique appeal points 37–41
self-disclosure, selective 129
self-presentation 21–2
self-protection 199–211
self-reflection 36
self-respect 52
self-rewards 71–2, 78–9
self-talk 100–1
self-trust 52
selling mode
  signs of 61
  stepping in and out of 60–1
  see also Commercial Cross-over Scripts
sentence fillers 158
'SHOUTING' 169
shyness 22, 84, 96
signatures, email 169–70
sins of networking 50
sitting positions 160
small talk 128–9, 140–4, 188, 242, 246
snide people 200
social life 231–2
social skills 10, 32
Sohn, Adam 256
spam 69, 170
special interest groups 233
speed networking 105
spongers 200
sports clubs 233
Stone, Carole 185, 224
Stone, Glenda 185, 187, 196
strategic alliances 26
strategic networking 15–17, 261–4
stress 87, 138
subconscious mind 109–10
success 20
summarising 137
super-confidence 22
superiority, illusions of 81–2
support 89–91
sympathy, inviting 86

talking points 124, 247
talks 222–3
technical skills 37, 39
telephone skills 179–80
testimonials 56–7
Teten, David 186
time management 264
Toastmasters 223, 260
training programmes 257, 259–60
trust 47–50
  benevolence-based 76
  and reputation 212
  self-trust 52
  testing for 130–1, 189–90

unconscious networking 15, **16**
unique appeal points (UAPs) 37–40
unique selling points (USPs) 37
unpredictability 93–4

vision statements 262
visualisation 21, 65–7, 155–6
voice 144–5, 160, 180
voluntary organisations 233–4

walks 160
Wallflowers 108
weaknesses
  accepting and controlling 41–3
  rectifying 82–3
  sharing 85–6, 191
web cameras 179

web design software 177
web hosting 177
web logs 173–6, 236
websites 17, 176–8, 230
white lies 102
Wilde, Oscar 212
win/win activities 154, 202
Wise Owl Know-how *see* knowledge base
Women in Business groups 17, 185
Wood, Derek 24
Wordsworth, William 65, 66–7
work settings 229–30
writing skills 222, 257
written information, processing 32–3

Zoominfo 239